W9-AEY-810

DISCARD

THE IMPORTANCE OF

Paul McCartney

Paul McCartney

by Kate Boyes

LUCENT
BOOKS®

THOMSON
™
GALE

San Diego • Detroit • New York • San Francisco • Cleveland • New Haven, Conn. • Waterville, Maine • London • Munich

THOMSON

GALE

For the Alligators,
a band that rocked California in the 1970s

© 2004 by Lucent Books. Lucent Books is an imprint of The Gale Group, Inc.,
a division of Thomson Learning, Inc.

Lucent Books® and Thomson Learning™ are trademarks used herein under license.

For more information, contact
Lucent Books
27500 Drake Rd.
Farmington Hills, MI 48331-3535
Or you can visit our Internet site at http://www.gale.com

LIBRARY OF CONGRESS CATALOGING-IN-PUBLICATION DATA

Boyes, Kate.
  Paul McCartney / by Kate Boyes.
    v. cm. — (The importance of)
Includes bibliographical references (p.) and index.
Contents: A good knight in the kingdom of rock—Frontier childhood in
war-torn England—All he needed was music—Paying his dues—Climbing the ladder to
fame—Conquering the world with the Beatles—Mantras, money, marriage, and Paul's
mortality—One door closes, another opens—Spreading his wings.
  ISBN 1-59018-283-9 (hardback : alk. paper)
 1. McCartney, Paul—Juvenile literature. 2. Rock musicians—England—Biography—
Juvenile literature. [1. McCartney, Paul. 2. Musicians. 3. Composers. 4. Rock music.]
I. Title. II. Series.
  ML3930.M37B6 2004
  782.42166'092—dc21
                                                   2003002301

Printed in the United States of America

Contents

Foreword

THE IMPORTANCE OF biography series deals with individuals who have made a unique contribution to history. The editors of the series have deliberately chosen to cast a wide net and include people from all fields of endeavor. Individuals from politics, music, art, literature, philosophy, science, sports, and religion are all represented. In addition, the editors did not restrict the series to individuals whose accomplishments have helped change the course of history. Of necessity, this criterion would have eliminated many whose contribution was great, though limited. Charles Darwin, for example, was responsible for radically altering the scientific view of the natural history of the world. His achievements continue to impact the study of science today. Others, such as Chief Joseph of the Nez Percé, played a pivotal role in the history of their own people. While Joseph's influence does not extend much beyond the Nez Percé, his nonviolent resistance to white expansion and his continuing role in protecting his tribe and his homeland remain an inspiration to all.

These biographies are more than factual chronicles. Each volume attempts to emphasize an individual's contributions both in his or her own time and for posterity. For example, the voyages of Christopher Columbus opened the way to European colonization of the New World. Unquestionably, his encounter with the New World brought monumental changes to both Europe and the Americas in his day. Today, however, the broader impact of Columbus's voyages is being critically scrutinized. *Christopher Columbus,* as well as every biography in The Importance Of series, includes and evaluates the most recent scholarship available on each subject.

Each author includes a wide variety of primary and secondary source quotations to document and substantiate his or her work. All quotes are footnoted to show readers exactly how and where biographers derive their information, as well as provide stepping stones to further research. These quotations enliven the text by giving readers eyewitness views of the life and times of each individual covered in The Importance Of series.

Finally, each volume is enhanced by photographs, bibliographies, chronologies, and comprehensive indexes. For both the casual reader and the student engaged in research, The Importance Of biographies will be a fascinating adventure into the lives of people who have helped shape humanity's past and present, and who will continue to shape its future.

IMPORTANT DATES IN THE LIFE OF
PAUL MCCARTNEY

1942
James Paul McCartney
is born in Liverpool,
England, on June 18.

1957
Meets John Lennon and
begins playing with the
Quarry Men.

1956
His mother dies.

1971
Creates rock band Wings;
third child, Stella, is born.

1970
Releases first solo album;
the Beatles disband.

1969
Marries Linda Eastman and
adopts her child, Heather;
second child, Mary, is born.

1945	1950	1955	1960	1965	1970

1958
Brings George Harrison
into band.

1960
Performances with the Beatles
spark Beatlemania.

1962
Signs on manager, record
company, and drummer Ringo
Starr; releases first song with
the Beatles.

1966
The Beatles play
last tour concert.

1965
Receives MBE award
from Queen Elizabeth.

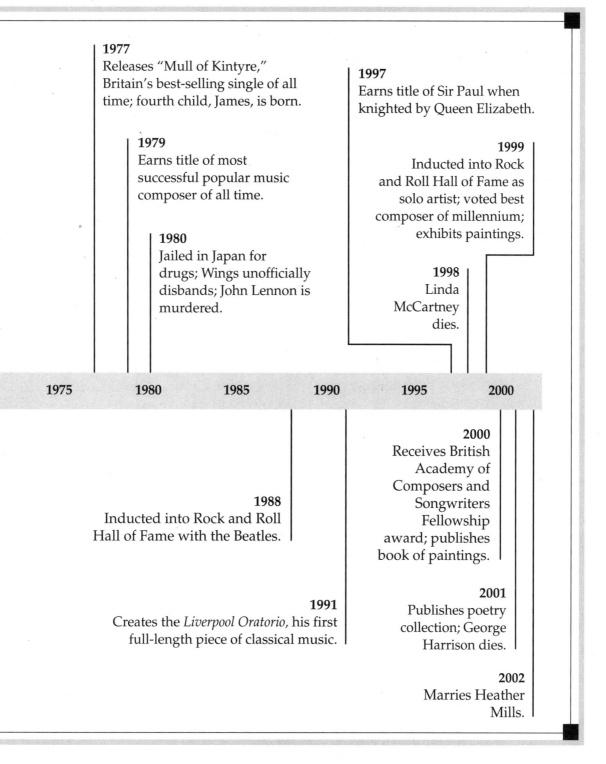

1977
Releases "Mull of Kintyre,"
Britain's best-selling single of all
time; fourth child, James, is born.

1979
Earns title of most
successful popular music
composer of all time.

1980
Jailed in Japan for
drugs; Wings unofficially
disbands; John Lennon is
murdered.

1997
Earns title of Sir Paul when
knighted by Queen Elizabeth.

1999
Inducted into Rock
and Roll Hall of Fame as
solo artist; voted best
composer of millennium;
exhibits paintings.

1998
Linda
McCartney
dies.

1975   1980   1985   1990   1995   2000

2000
Receives British
Academy of
Composers and
Songwriters
Fellowship
award; publishes
book of paintings.

1988
Inducted into Rock and Roll
Hall of Fame with the Beatles.

1991
Creates the *Liverpool Oratorio*, his first
full-length piece of classical music.

2001
Publishes poetry
collection; George
Harrison dies.

2002
Marries Heather
Mills.

A Good Knight in the Kingdom of Rock

I would say that it doesn't matter whether you're the king of a country or you're the Sultan of Brunei or you're a fabulous Beatle; it's what's inside that counts.

—George Harrison

Paul McCartney was waiting for his plane to take off from a New York City airport when the World Trade Center was attacked on September 11, 2001. Through his plane window, he watched the Twin Towers burn and collapse. McCartney says the image horrified him and "it will live with me forever." [1]

Several days later, he braved rain, smoke, and destruction to say a prayer at the edge of the attack site. Police officers recognized McCartney and gave him permission to enter ground zero, where the Twin Towers had stood. While there, he witnessed the rescue efforts of exhausted but dedicated firefighters and volunteers, whose hard work reminded him of his father's service as a fireman during World War II. When he climbed out of ground zero, he said, "I have great admiration for [their] courage." [2]

McCartney felt he needed to do something to honor the rescue workers. "Singing is the only way I know how to help," [3] he said. He decided to organize a massive ben-

efit concert to raise money for the workers, and a few phone calls started the ball rolling. The concert, held in October 2001 at Madison Square Garden, featured top performers: Jon Bon Jovi, Destiny's Child, Adam Sandler, Billy Joel, Halle Berry, Mick Jagger, Kid Rock, and Harrison Ford. The event raised over $30 million.

Paul McCartney managed to organize the concert and attract a cast of stars because he is one of the world's most popular and successful musicians. For over forty years, McCartney's songs have set the standard of artistic excellence for rock music. His work and the honors he has received for it have brought him fame, which he often uses, as he did in New York City, to make a positive difference in the world.

ONE OF THE FAB FOUR

McCartney rose to fame with the Beatles, a rock band that also included John Lennon, George Harrison, and Ringo Starr. From 1962, when their first song hit the music charts, to 1970, when they disbanded, the Beatles set records for the most number one songs in the United States, the most number one albums in the United States, and the most consecutive number one songs in

Britain. The Beatles still hold these records, making them the most successful music group of all time. McCartney and Lennon, who wrote many of the Beatles' songs together, still hold the title of the most successful songwriting team in history.

For McCartney and his band mates, nicknamed the "Fab Four," setting records was not as important as making their audience happy. The Beatles were master crowd pleasers, inspiring fanatical devotion, known as "Beatlemania," in rock enthusiasts around the world. Fans broke through chain-link fences to be near the group, screamed so loud during concerts that the Beatles' singing often could not be heard, and fainted when they received autographs. The response to the group was so intense that John Lennon said, "I think The Beatles *were* a kind of religion and that

Paul epitomised The Beatles and the . . . hero image."[4]

FLYING HIGH, WITH AND WITHOUT WINGS

Record-setting music and crowd-pleasing performances brought McCartney many honors with the Beatles, and he continued to win acclaim for his music after the group disbanded. The sheer number of his hit singles and albums since then have earned him the title of the most successful popular music composer of all time.

Music critics believe Paul McCartney will hold that title for many years, and for an important reason: Most musicians do not produce work for as long as he has, especially in the physically and mentally exhausting

Paul McCartney and a New York policeman salute the crowd at a benefit concert McCartney organized to raise money for emergency personnel in the aftermath of the September 11 terrorist attacks.

field of rock music. McCartney has accumulated an extensive list of records set, titles earned, and honors won because he is talented and has a strong will to succeed, and these traits have allowed his career to span more than four decades. Biographer Chet Flippo says that, considering the high rate of death and desertion in the realm of rock 'n' roll, McCartney is "the most celebrated, most successful, and richest of all the rock 'n' rollers who have ever lived" and "is now left as the only genuine member of rock's royalty."[5]

GIVING SOMETHING BACK

Royalty status in the realm of rock 'n' roll has made McCartney the richest enter-

tainer in Britain, and he has used his fortune to help improve the world around him. His love of the arts led him to establish a performing arts school in his old hometown of Liverpool. He supports human rights groups and the anti-landmine campaign. He donates money to animal rights groups and has become a vegetarian as an outgrowth of his concerns about the ethical treatment of animals. He is an avid environmentalist, providing valuable funding and publicity for groups working to improve the health of the Earth.

Recently, he has focused many of his charitable efforts on improving the health of humans. In memory of his mother, his wife, and his former band mate George Harrison, all of whom died from cancer, McCartney has contributed millions of dollars to keep

The Beatles (from left, Ringo Starr, John Lennon, Paul McCartney and George Harrison) proudly display medals that the Queen of England awarded them in recognition of their contribution to the arts.

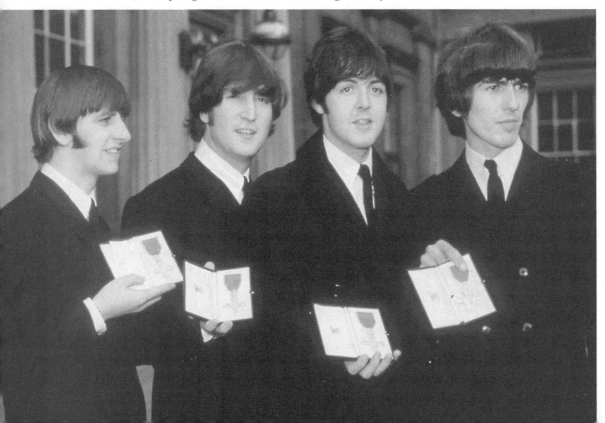

McCartney escorts Queen Elizabeth through the Liverpool Institute for the Performing Arts, a college McCartney established to promote the arts.

health clinics open and to support cancer research.

ARISE, SIR PAUL

McCartney's willingness to help others led to one of his highest honors: In 1997, he was made a knight. This is a rare award given by Britain's royal family to people who have shown long and distinguished service to the country and to humanity.

At the investiture ceremony, McCartney knelt before Queen Elizabeth while she gave him a medal and then tapped him on the shoulder with a sword. The sword she used had belonged to Edward the Confessor, who was England's king almost one thousand years ago. McCartney was impressed by the event. "This is one of the best days of my life," he said. "To come from a terraced house in Liverpool to this house [Buckingham Palace] is quite a journey and I am immensely proud."[6]

Chapter 1

Frontier Childhood in War-Torn England

We always felt like a pioneer family in a wagon train.

—Paul McCartney

In 1942, Jim and Mary McCartney were struggling to survive World War II. Their hometown of Liverpool, England, was bombed frequently, and they lived next to the mass graves where victims of bombing attacks were buried. Air-raid sirens announcing the attacks kept Mary, who was pregnant, awake night after night. She could not turn on a light when she woke; even the spark of a match might provide a target for enemy planes flying overhead. She could only wait in total darkness for the sound—and the destruction—of exploding bombs.

Her husband, Jim, was often away from home at night. Jim McCartney was forty, too old to be a soldier. Mary helped the war effort by caring for neighbors as a part-time visiting nurse, and Jim wanted to help his country, too. During the day, he built engines for military vehicles; after work, he served as a volunteer firefighter. The scream of air-raid sirens at night was his signal to join other volunteers in putting out fires caused by bombs. On quiet nights, he stood watch on a rooftop, ready to warn neighbors of attacks.

Jim was standing watch on June 18, 1942, when Mary gave birth to a boy in Walton Hospital, where she had worked as a nurse. The new parents named their son James Paul McCartney. He was called Paul by family, friends, and, in decades to come, by music lovers around the world.

AFTER THE WAR

By the time World War II ended in 1945, Jim and Mary had two children, three-year-old Paul and his nineteen-month-old brother, Michael. While the war had killed or wounded thousands of people in their hometown of Liverpool, the McCartneys had escaped injury. Now they faced the challenges of living in a city severely damaged by war.

Although financial hardships were widespread in England at that time, the city of Liverpool was hit particularly hard. Bombs had destroyed dozens of stores and factory buildings in the city, and jobs at those businesses were lost. Many people had trouble finding work. Biographer Ross Benson says of postwar Liverpool that "the city crumbled away to become one of the poorest in Europe."[7]

Before the war, Jim McCartney had worked as a cotton salesman, a good job with a decent salary. After the war, the cotton industry faltered, and Jim, too, became unemployed. He was relieved when he finally found work, first as a janitor and then as a mechanic. However, his salary was far less than before the war.

Mary wanted to stay at home with her young sons, but she took a part-time job as a visiting nurse to help bring in a little extra money. When Jim's salary was cut, Mary returned to nursing full-time as a midwife, caring for pregnant patients to help support the family.

ON THE FRONTIER

In addition to securing employment, the McCartney family, like most in postwar Liverpool, faced the challenge of finding a decent home. Many of the McCartneys' neighbors lived without running water or electricity in houses damaged by bombs. The homes of at least ten thousand families had been turned into piles of rubble during air raids. Whole city blocks of badly damaged buildings had been torn down because they were a safety hazard.

Mary's full-time nursing job included, as a benefit, a home in one of the new housing

Six-year-old Paul McCartney poses with his little brother Mike. The McCartneys were poor, and they faced many hardships in postwar Liverpool.

THE BOMBING OF LIVERPOOL

Paul McCartney's hometown of Liverpool, England, suffered major damage during World War II, as biographer Barry Miles recounts in Paul McCartney: Many Years from Now:

During World War II Liverpool suffered terribly from the German air raids: from the night of 17 August 1940 until 10 January 1942 there were sixty-eight raids and over five hundred air-raid warnings. Every night thousands of people huddled together in basements and bomb shelters as high-explosive, incendiary and parachute bombs rained down upon the city, killing 2650, seriously injuring over 2000 others and leaving much of the city centre in ruins. The dead were buried in mass graves in Anfield cemetery. Over 10,000 of the homes in Liverpool were completely destroyed and two-thirds of all homes were seriously damaged.

Children sit among the rubble of their ruined Liverpool home, one of thousands destroyed by Nazi bombing raids.

developments being constructed around the edges of Liverpool. The houses and apartments were built in open fields or on sites that had been hit by bombs. Even though Paul was young when his family moved to their new home, he recalls his early days there: "We played on bomb-sites a lot and I grew up thinking the word 'bomb-site' almost meant 'playground.'"[8]

Paul's mother cared for the pregnant residents of these developments until local clinics could be built. Mary worked long hours in difficult conditions for the privilege of having a house. A patient might go into labor at any time, and Mary had to be there to deliver the baby no matter what the hour. Paul recalls one night as an example: "The streets were thick with snow, it was about three in the morning, and [my mother] got up and went out on her bike with the little brown wicker basket on the front, into the dark, . . . cycling off down the [road] to deliver a baby somewhere."[9]

CONSTANTLY MAKING NEW FRIENDS

Whenever a new housing development opened on the outskirts of Liverpool, Mary was sent there to work. This meant the family moved frequently. "No sooner would we be established in one house than we would be moved to a new one," Paul says. "We'd live there for a while and then it would be 'whipcrack away,' and we were moving again."[10]

The McCartney family moved seven times during the next ten years. Paul's brother, Michael, grumbled about the frequent moves,

but Paul did not seem to mind too much. Each time the family moved, their house was nicer, with bigger rooms or newer carpets. Every move gave Paul the opportunity to explore a new area of the city. Spending so much of his childhood on the move made extended world tours with the Beatles seem natural to Paul when he was an adult. Also, the frequent moves taught Paul that he had to be outgoing if he wanted to make new friends, a skill he would use throughout his life.

THE FIRST AWARD

Moving as frequently as the McCartneys did meant Paul often attended new schools, but he had no problem making the transitions. He was a good student, and he worked hard.

Hard work brought Paul his first award, a writing prize. Queen Elizabeth II ascended to the throne of England in 1952 when her father, King George VI, died. Students throughout the country entered essays in a competition to celebrate her coronation ceremony, which was held in 1953. Paul won the prize for his age group. "It was my first prize ever," Paul recalls. "I had to go up, and the [Mayor of Liverpool] gave me the prize. It was the first time I ever felt my knees go to rubber."[11]

The prize included two books: one about the queen and one about any subject Paul wanted. He chose a book about modern art, a subject that fascinated him. Paul says the book was "fabulous. It was just lots and lots of pictures; people like Victor Pasmore, Salvador Dali, Picasso, and a lot of artists I hadn't heard of. I'd always been attracted to art. I used to draw a lot."[12]

OFF TO THE INNY

That same year, 1953, Paul took a test given to all students in England when they reached eleven years old. The test results determined what type of school the students would attend during their teen years. Students who scored high enough could attend institutions, much like high schools in the United States, that prepared them to study at universities.

Paul scored high enough to be accepted into the Liverpool Institute, nicknamed the "Inny," which took only the city's most ad-

vanced students. Jim and Mary McCartney were thrilled; they wanted Paul to receive a good education, and they knew that students from the Liverpool Institute often went on to attend the best universities in England.

Paul was pleased with his test results, but he was not as thrilled as his parents about the institute. He had to study harder there to keep up with his classes. Courses included not only the usual subjects taught in high school but also more difficult subjects, such as classical literature and Latin. Still, he had learned to get along in any situation, and he

LEARNING RELIGIOUS TOLERANCE AT THE DOCKS

In The Beatles Anthology, *Paul McCartney explains the religious lessons he learned by hanging around the docks in his hometown of Liverpool:*

I developed my religious philosophy at the pierhead. . . . You always had the Catholics arguing with the Protestants. The Protestants would say, "What my friend over there is telling you is all wrong. There is no such thing as mortal sin, you're not born a sinner." And then the Catholic guy would start up: "My friend over there doesn't know that there *is* such a thing as mortal sin, and if you don't get rid of your guilt you will burn in hell and damnation." They couldn't get it together, even though they were both Christians. The Irish problem, the Middle-Eastern problem—it's all down to that.

I was exposed to many religious arguments on the pierhead, and I came to the conclusion that "God" is just the word "good" with the "o" taken out, and "Devil" is the word "evil" with a "D" added. Really, all that people have done throughout history is to personify the two forces of Good and Evil. And although they've given them many names—like Jehovah or Allah—I've got a feeling that it's all the same.

did well at the Inny. His favorite teacher, Alan Durband, recalls, "He was always respected by the other boys. . . . I think he was privately what he became publicly—the person always ready with a witty comment: he would make all his mates and peers collapse with laughter at the [whispered] remark. . . . It was very much the Liverpool wit."[13]

"MOTHER NATURE'S SON"

After school, Paul spent as much time as possible outside. Often, he worked outdoors with his father, who always kept a garden when the family lived in a house with a yard. Jim McCartney taught Paul how to grow vegetables and flowers organically by adding horse manure to the soil. The police in England still rode horses at that time, so Paul's father would send him off to the police station with a bucket to collect manure. This was not Paul's favorite job, but he did not mind it too much—as long as his friends did not see what was in the bucket.

Jim McCartney's fondness for nature helped Paul develop a love of the outdoors. Sometimes Jim led the family on long walks through the woods. Also, he took his wife and sons to a rural camp to spend their holidays. Remembering his father's early influence, Paul said, "This is where my love of the country came from."[14]

The fields around Paul's house were full of wildlife, and he lived close to the woods and the river. When he was not gardening, he enjoyed playing in the woods with his brother and friends or taking long walks alone and sitting by the river with only the water creatures and a book to keep him company. Paul's outdoor experiences inspired several of the songs he wrote later in life. He says, "I was always able to take my bike and in five minutes I'd be in quite deep countryside. . . . This is what I was writing about in 'Mother Nature's Son' [which is] basically a heart-felt song about my child-of-nature leanings."[15]

A TOUGH HOMETOWN

Spending days at the Liverpool Institute and after-school hours in the woods allowed Paul to escape some of the problems that plagued his neighbors. The new housing developments where the McCartneys lived were often bleak and ugly. Neither the McCartneys nor most of their neighbors owned cars, and they felt isolated from the shops, churches, and schools in the center of Liverpool, where they had lived before the war.

Bleak surroundings, isolation, poverty, and frustration often led to violence in these neighborhoods. Paul was mugged and robbed there when he was ten years old. He recalls that gangs were also a problem in the housing developments. Most of the violence occurred when gangs from nearby

districts entered his neighborhood, leading to fights between the local group and the intruders. He explains, "And suddenly the word would go round, because it was like a frontier town in the Wild West: 'The lads from Garston are coming!' . . . and our bigger guys didn't run. They would go and meet them. It was very very real. It was serious fighting."[16]

Living in the housing developments taught Paul some valuable lessons. He learned that tense situations can often be diffused with smiles and cheery words and that humor can be an effective tool for dealing with problems. Most important, Paul learned to value his close, protective family.

A CLOSE CIRCLE OF LOVE

Paul's family was the solid rock that kept his childhood secure. Jim and Mary McCartney worked to create a happy home life for their children.

Jim and Mary gave Paul his first lessons in tolerance. Mary was Catholic, Jim was Protestant, and both were Irish. Deadly battles between Catholics and Protestants were prevalent in Ireland at that time, and fights between members of the two religions were so widespread and intense that Mary's family was shocked when she married a Protestant. And yet, Paul never saw his parents argue about their religious differences.

Paul's extended family also played an important role in keeping his childhood secure. Both Jim and Mary McCartney came from large families, and Paul and his brother were surrounded with aunts, un-

McCartney learned to play piano by watching his father, who loved to perform songs at family gatherings.

cles, and cousins. Family members watched the boys if Jim and Mary were busy with work. Although Paul describes his family as average or ordinary, he says, "I've been around the world a few times, to all its little pockets, and . . . I've never met anyone more soulful, more intelligent, more kind, more filled with common sense, than [my family] in Liverpool."[17]

THE MUSICAL MCCARTNEYS

When Paul's many relatives gathered, music filled the McCartney house. Paul's grand-

father had played in several bands, and, during the 1930s, Jim McCartney had been the leader of his own band. Several of Paul's uncles and cousins also played instruments. As a result, McCartney family parties were lively. Paul especially liked the parties his family held every New Year's Eve, when all of his relatives paused at midnight to listen to the tunes of a roving bagpipe player.

Paul's father played the piano at these gatherings. The family's old piano had spent World War II hidden behind a barrier of sandbags in an air-raid shelter. It sounded good to young Paul, who was introduced to music through his father's piano playing

McCartney's two-year-old daughter, Mary, demonstrates an early interest in music. Mary was named after McCartney's mother, who died of cancer when he was fourteen.

and who later learned to play the instrument by watching his father. "I have some lovely childhood memories of lying on the floor and listening to my dad play," Paul says. "To this day, I have a deep love for the piano."[18]

TRAGEDY STRIKES

By 1955, the McCartney family had finally achieved some comfort and stability. Jim

and Mary's salaries covered family expenses and provided for a few luxuries, such as a television set. Paul and his brother both attended the Liverpool Institute. The family moved to a nice house at 20 Forthlin Road. This house was a major step up for the McCartneys because, for the first time, they had an indoor toilet.

Mary McCartney began feeling pain in her chest not long after the move. When the pain became too uncomfortable, she took an over-the-counter medicine from the drug store. However, the pain became unbearable in the late summer of 1956. Mary finally talked to her doctor, who discovered that she had breast cancer.

At that time, cancer was not a topic discussed with young people. Paul and his brother were told only that their mother was ill. When Mary entered the hospital for surgery to remove the cancer, they were sent to stay with relatives.

The operation was not a success because the cancer had spread throughout much of Mary's body. When it was clear that she would not recover and was near death, Paul and his brother were brought to the hospital to see her. "It was a huge shock to us," Paul recalls, "because suddenly she was very ill, and we were very young. There was a little bit of blood on the sheets and it was really creepy for us at that age. Nobody was holding out much hope for her. This was very scary." [19]

At that time, Paul had no idea how hard Mary had worked to make their family life warm and happy. It took years for Paul to understand her sacrifices. "She was a re-

ally wonderful woman and really did pull the family along," Paul says. "She was, as so many women are, the unsung leader of the family." [20]

THE CIRCLE IS BROKEN

On October 31, 1956, Mary McCartney died. Paul and his brother learned of her death from the aunt with whom they were staying.

Over a decade later, Paul wrote "Let It Be," a song inspired by his mother. The song is about finding peace in troubled times, but Paul felt no peace on the day his mother died. He cried and prayed for her return. As biographer Chris Salewicz has noted, "Mary McCartney's death was the most devastating experience of [Paul's] young life, its dark paralyzing shock waves sweeping with resounding effect over all his succeeding years. Ultimately, it was to prove the principal motivating factor behind all that he became." [21]

Chapter

2 All He Needed Was . . . Music

The rock and roll bug . . . had bitten me.

—Paul McCartney

After the shock of his mother's death wore off, fourteen-year-old Paul McCartney stopped praying for her return. He handled the loss by hiding his grief and withdrawing from the world. "I carried on," Paul says. "I learnt to put a shell around me at that age."[22]

Paul began to skip school. He stopped hanging around with friends. With his mother's laughter gone from the McCartney home, Paul spent most of his free time in his room, closed off from a house that was suddenly too quiet. He seldom talked to his father, Jim, or to his brother, Michael, who says, "I had better conversations with brick walls around this period."[23]

TRYING TO FILL THE SILENCE

To fill the hours in his room, Paul turned to music. His father had strung wires from the family's radio set, on the main floor of the house, to the upstairs bedrooms. There were not many music programs on the air in 1956, but, by using headphones, Paul was able to find a clear signal from the British Broadcasting Corporation (BBC), England's only radio station at that time.

Although the BBC aired so-called popular music, it was not the kind Paul really liked. Included in the lineup were big band and vaudeville numbers as well as movie and theater show tunes made popular by singers such as Doris Day, Pat Boone, and Frank Sinatra. As music historian Ray Coleman explains, it was "the sort of music Jim McCartney might enjoy, but with minimal teenage appeal."[24]

ROCK ON RADIO LUXEMBOURG

The music Paul craved most was a new style called rock 'n' roll that had just started to cross the ocean from the United States. In 1955, Paul had fallen in love with rock 'n' roll when he heard "Rock Around the Clock." "I remember watching [television] and seeing Bill Haley [and the Comets] perform the song," Paul says, "and it was the first piece of music that ever sent a tingle up my spine."[25] Then, in the spring of 1956, Elvis Presley's "Heartbreak Hotel" reached England and created the same frenzy of excitement it had set off among teenagers in America.

By the final months of 1956, the new musical style had become so popular that ten of the top twenty songs on the British charts were classified as rock 'n' roll. But the BBC would not play those songs.

One radio station in Europe played new music and had a signal just barely strong enough for Paul to pick up in Liverpool. The station, Radio Luxembourg, broadcast its popular music shows in English each evening, creating a large teenage audience in the United Kingdom. In his room at night, Paul tuned in to hear the recorded music of Elvis Presley, Fats Domino, Bill Haley,

Teenagers dance to the new sound of rock 'n' roll. The young Paul McCartney listened to American artists such as Elvis Presley and Little Richard.

Buddy Holly, Little Richard, and Chuck Berry. Many of the early rock 'n' roll songs Paul strained to hear through his headphones in the mid-1950s have since become classics: "Blueberry Hill," "Be Bop A-Lula," "Long Tall Sally," and "Blue Suede Shoes."

THAT NEW-STYLE ROCK 'N' ROLL

Rock 'n' roll music appealed to Paul and to millions of other teens because it combined the best elements of swing, jazz, rhythm and blues, country, gospel, and folk music, creating a new sound through that fusion. Most songs had a quick tempo, giving them a high-energy quality that made listeners want to dance. The strong beat created a solid rhythm—also good for dancing. The combination of drums, guitar, bass, saxophone, and piano gave rock 'n' roll a sound that was not as heavy as big bands or orchestras. Even the slow rock songs were powerful: The lyrics spoke honestly of raw emotion, and the tunes were mellow but not overly sweet, as were so many traditional love songs.

Something else made rock 'n' roll irresistible, especially to young people—the excitement lead singers created with their distinctive presentation styles. The wailing, crooning, snarling, screaming, prancing, and hip gyrating of these singers thrilled teenagers of Paul McCartney's generation, who were used to neat, predictable, and completely respectable musicians. As Paul says, "before the mid-1950s, you were looking at a [Frank] Sinatra-type person as the most rocking you were gonna get. Then suddenly Elvis arrived and Chuck Berry

... and all the guys. From then on, that was the whole direction."[26]

AN UPSIDE-DOWN GUITAR

Listening to rock 'n' roll music helped Paul pass the long hours in his room, and that satisfied him—for a while. But he came from a family of musicians, and soon he longed to play the songs he heard.

Paul had to overcome several obstacles before he could play rock music. First, he needed an instrument. He had received a trumpet for his fourteenth birthday, but the instrument had never captured his interest. Also, he wanted an instrument he could play while singing. Eventually, his father gave him permission to trade the trumpet for an inexpensive acoustic guitar.

Now Paul faced another obstacle: He could not read music. His father could not help him because even though Jim McCartney played the trumpet and piano, he had never learned to read music. Paul says he ended up teaching himself to play by ear, the same way his father had learned. To do this, Paul had to listen carefully to a song being broadcast on the radio or watch closely as another guitarist played a song, and then try to recreate it one chord at a time. The process was slow, difficult, and often frustrating, but by listening to a song again and again he could figure out all the chords.

Paul soon discovered another difficulty he needed to overcome. Although he watched closely when other guitarists played songs, he had trouble recreating the chords they used. He put his fingers on the

"Something Wild and Physical"

Rock 'n' roll music was a welcome relief for Paul McCartney and millions of other young people during the dreary post-World War II era, as Malcolm Doney explains in Lennon and McCartney, *his examination of the composing team's relationship:*

[As] rationing gave way to a burgeoning consumer boom, young people shook off the past their parents tried to hand down to them. They wanted excitement, freedom—a good time. Shuffling about on the dance floor . . . did not fit into their aspirations.

But rock'n'roll did. When the first raucous sound of Bill Haley and The Comets filtered across the Atlantic, it meshed well with the feelings of the young. Here was something wild and physical enough for them to launch themselves into. Then came the teddy boys in their long Edwardian-style drape coats with narrow lapels and velvet collars, drain-pipe trousers ending just short of the ankle from whence peered day-glo socks. . . .

It was these Fifties creatures . . . who first took rock'n'roll to their hearts. Their looks and behaviour were a slap in the face to their parents' generation—an inarticulate rebellion against the more prudent values that had come through the war years.

guitar strings in the same places they did, but the sound he produced was not the same. The problem was simple: Paul was left-handed. To make his chords sound just like those of right-handed guitarists, McCartney turned his guitar upside down and reversed the position of his fingers on the strings.

Music Becomes an Addiction

As soon as Paul received his guitar he began to play it constantly, filling his room with the upbeat sound of rock music. When he emerged from his room, the gui-

tar came too so he could practice it wherever he went. Even excursions to the bathroom turned into practice time when Paul discovered the echo effect he could achieve by playing the guitar in that small room.

His father and his brother, Michael, thought the guitar was Paul's substitute for Mary McCartney. Michael thought that it was a very odd substitute. "It was just after Mother's death that it started," Michael says. "It became an obsession. It took over his whole life. You lose a mother—and you find a guitar?"[27]

Paul began to skip school more often so he could practice music, and his grades

McCartney taught himself to play guitar, and he practiced for hours at a time. His passion for music led him to neglect his studies.

dropped. The reports he brought home from school were no longer glowing. According to McCartney biographer Ray Coleman, Paul's report cards now "contained comments like: 'If he doesn't im-

prove I shall punish him' . . . and: 'He is the biggest disappointment in the class.'" [28]

Finally, Paul failed some classes and had to repeat a grade. He was not troubled by this. In fact, repeating classes became part of his scheme to delay the realities of adult life so he could focus a few more years of his life on music. He developed the plan after seeing a twenty-four-year-old student at a local school. Paul says the incident "planted the idea in my mind, 'Ah, you can hang on till you're twenty-four, then you've got to get a job or something. Then the game is up.'"[29]

DESPERATELY SEEKING SONGS

Paul's obsession with music hurt his grades, but it also had a positive effect: Eventually, it prompted him to leave the seclusion of his room in search of songs. A rock 'n' roll song might be aired on the radio only a few times each week, making it hard for Paul to learn how to play it by ear. He really needed to listen to a recording over and over again to pick out the chords. But records and the machines on which they were played were too expensive for the McCartneys now that the family had only one wage earner.

Even people with more money than Paul's family had trouble purchasing recordings of American rock 'n' roll music in England, or in most parts of Europe, at that time. Today, a song released in the United States is often available for sale immediately throughout the world. In the mid-1950s, a best-selling song from America might not be broadcast in Europe until weeks after it hit the U.S. charts. A recording of that song might not show up in European music stores for months.

However, young people in Liverpool had an advantage over those elsewhere in England when it came to obtaining rock 'n' roll records from America. The city was a major shipping port. Many Liverpudlians, as people from Liverpool call themselves, worked on ships that carried cargo back and forth to the United States, or they helped load and unload ships at the docks.

FORGETTING THE "ACADEMIC THINGS"

In Paul McCartney: Many Years from Now, *a biography by Barry Miles, McCartney describes his increasing interest in artistic subjects as a teenager and the negative reactions of his teachers:*

I nearly did very well at . . . school but I started to get interested in art instead of academic subjects. Then I started to see pictures of Elvis, and . . . hear the records. . . . And so the academic things were forgotten.

The words they used in their end-of-term reports: "If he would only buckle down . . ." and you'd go, "No! No! Get out of my life! I hate you! You should say I'm great. I've got to take this home, you know." If I had buckled down, it could have worked out that way, but I'm glad it didn't, of course. There was always the great pull of the other stuff: show business, music, art, the other stuff.

Crew members bought records while in U.S. ports, then sold the records to dockhands in Liverpool or passed the records along to their friends and family.

This was the era of the record party, when young people gathered at the homes of friends who had both rock 'n' roll records and a gramophone, an early form of record player. Most teens owned only a handful of records, but those few and precious songs would be repeated many times during a party. To have fun and to learn new songs, Paul sought out record parties.

THE PICNIC THAT CHANGED HIS LIFE

On July 6, 1957, Paul went to a different type of gathering, a church picnic, in search of company. He intended to find a girl who might want to go out on a date, but none of the girls there were interested in him. However, a group called the Quarry Men provided music for the event, and Paul was drawn to the group because the leader was a guitar player.

The group played skiffle, a musical style popular in England at that time. The style was a blend of traditional, jazz, blues, and folk music, and many skiffle players used simple instruments they made from materials found around the house, such as washtubs, broomsticks, and wooden boxes. Skiffle appealed to young people because it had some of the same roots as rock 'n' roll music but did not require the expensive saxophones and electric guitars often used by rock players.

Members of the Quarry Men were teenagers, like Paul, and their instruments were of even lower quality than his cheap guitar. No one in the group was a skilled musician. Even the group's leader was a novice, although it was hard to tell if he messed up the words and chords of the songs he played because he had little experience or because he was drunk.

During a break between sets, the leader of the group started playing rock 'n' roll tunes. Paul introduced himself to the guitar player, John Lennon. Paul discovered that John was as passionate about rock music as he was. John explained his love of rock 'n' roll: "When I heard it I dropped everything else. It was instinctive. Rock 'n' roll music gets right through to you without having to go through your brain. [It] goes right to the gut!"[30]

Paul was excited to find someone who shared his love for rock music. He spent a few hours with the group that afternoon, playing rock songs and showing John and the other Quarry Men how to tune a guitar.

PART OF THE GROUP

John Lennon was impressed with Paul McCartney but was hesitant to ask him to join the Quarry Men. Paul was fifteen, much younger than the other members of the group. Also, John was concerned that Paul might want to take over his role as group leader. "It went through my head," John recalled later, "that I'd have to keep him in line if I let him join."[31]

The Quarry Men needed someone with solid skills. The group also needed stabil-

Paul McCartney and John Lennon shared a love for music and songwriting. Lennon invited McCartney to join his band because of McCartney's strong musical ability.

ity: People tended to join for a few weeks and then quit abruptly when they discovered that practicing music was hard work. Paul had taught himself how to play the guitar; that proved he was willing to work hard. According to John, Paul "was good, so he was worth having. He also looked like Elvis. I dug him." [32]

John's desire to have a good group overcame his concerns about Paul, and after a few weeks, he decided to allow Paul to join the group. Paul jumped at the chance to be in a real band, and he began practicing with John and the other members of the group. By the fall of 1957, Paul was performing with the Quarry Men in public.

THE MUSICAL TWINS

Other members of the Quarry Men came and went over the next nine months, but

MEETING JOHN LENNON

In Blackbird: The Life and Times of Paul McCartney, *biographer Geoffrey Giuliano describes the first time Paul McCartney met John Lennon and McCartney's roundabout invitation to join the Quarry Men:*

[Within] minutes things heated up when it was discovered that McCartney not only played a pretty mean left-handed guitar, but wonder of wonders, could actually correctly tune one as well. . . .

McCartney further wowed the often standoffish Lennon by jotting down the somewhat convoluted lyrics to singer Eddie Cochran's classic, "Twenty Flight Rock," as well as Gene Vincent's crazy "Be-Bop-A-Lula." [McCartney] recounts what happened next: "I met them in the church hall. We talked and then I picked up a guitar lying there and started to play. . . . I suppose I was showing off a bit. I knew all the words and they didn't. That was big currency. Then I went through all the stuff I knew. John seemed quite impressed. . . . "

Two weeks later . . . McCartney ran into [a member of the Quarry Men] who offhandedly announced that John had been talking about him and wondered if he would like to join the band. Delicately balancing against the curb on his bike, McCartney reflected for a moment or two and then replied simply, "Okay then. See you."

Paul McCartney and John Lennon remained. The schools they attended were located near each other, allowing Paul and John to practice music together between classes—when they chose to attend school. They often skipped school and hung out at Paul's place; with his father away at work, they were free to raid the refrigerator, smoke stolen cigarettes, write songs, and play music. John began sharing the leadership of the Quarry Men with Paul. Remembering this period in their friendship, Paul says, "John and I were perfect for each other."[33]

Differences in their experiences and personalities made them seem an unlikely pair. Paul came from the working class; John came from the middle class. Paul had been a good student before his mother died; John had disliked school from the beginning. Paul tried to be pleasant, friendly, and responsible. According to biographer Ross Benson, John "was rough, cruel and iconoclastic, . . . a headstrong rebel without a cause intent on causing offence."[34]

However, both Paul and John were inspired by traditional music and folk music. Both had found that the tunes, lyrics, and rhythms of rock 'n' roll music resonated inside them. Both enjoyed writing songs. And both wanted to do nothing else with their lives but play music. Paul and John were so close that they called themselves the "Nerk Twins" when they performed as a duo, and Paul often described the two of them as being more like twin brothers than friends.

THE BOND GROWS CLOSER

In the summer of 1958, John's mother was struck and killed by a drunk driver when she was on her way to visit him. John was heartbroken. His reaction to the death of his mother was similar to Paul's reaction when Mary McCartney died. For over a year, John withdrew from the world, even disbanding the Quarry Men. He skipped school more often. He spent most of his time alone.

Paul visited John whenever he wanted company. He also practiced music with John and encouraged him to write songs. Paul became a true friend, one of the few people John spent time with during his year of mourning. By the summer of the following year, 1959, the bond between Paul McCartney and John Lennon seemed unbreakable.

3 Paying His Dues

As kids from the sticks there was no guarantee that we were going to make it.

—Paul McCartney

Paul McCartney continued to develop his musical skills after the original Quarry Men disbanded in 1958. He practiced guitar with John Lennon whenever possible. When Lennon wanted to be alone, McCartney played with a young guitarist named George Harrison.

McCartney had met Harrison while riding the bus to the Liverpool Institute, which they both attended, and they had become good friends. Both of them came from working-class families. Also, Harrison's father had been an avid musician, like McCartney's father, and he supported his son's interest in music. Most important, Harrison shared McCartney's fascination with rock music.

Harrison was one of the lucky Liverpool teens with a source of American records and access to a record player. Listening to records, taking guitar lessons, and practicing constantly helped him develop skills the Quarry Men needed, and McCartney introduced him to the group in 1958. Harrison was almost three years younger than Lennon, who thought of him as a little kid.

However, Harrison knew more chords than anyone else in the group.

In the summer of 1959, Lennon decided to create a new Quarry Men, which would be more serious about developing as professional musicians and would play less skiffle and more rock 'n' roll. He wanted McCartney in the group because McCartney was serious about being a musician and had become a good friend. Lennon planned to exclude everyone else. However, McCartney urged him to include Harrison because he could play solos, something neither McCartney nor Lennon could do. Lennon agreed, and a new three-member Quarry Men band was formed.

PARLORS AND BOMB SHELTERS

In America, fledgling rock groups of the 1950s and 1960s tended to practice in garages so their loud music would not annoy family members. This earned them the nickname "garage bands." In Liverpool, where most people did not own cars and most houses had no garage, finding a practice space for the Quarry Men was a challenge.

When the group practiced at Lennon's house, his Aunt Mimi made them play on the porch. The Harrison home was often too crowded to accommodate a band. McCartney's father encouraged the group to practice in the parlor of the McCartneys' 20 Forthlin Road house. However, they had to keep the sound low if McCartney's father or brother were home—not easy to do while wailing through "Long Tall Sally."

The Quarry Men became experts at finding empty places in which to practice. Sometimes, they used old World War II bomb shelters, which had the advantage of being almost soundproof. When they were desperate, they broke into the houses of people they knew when those people were not home. The band would crawl in

George Harrison, John Lennon, and Paul McCartney stand outside McCartney's home in Liverpool, where the Quarry Men often practiced.

through an open window, play music for a few hours, help themselves to snacks, and then clean up before sneaking back out again.

GETTING GIGS AND GETTING BIGGER

All the hours of practice McCartney and the other Quarry Men put in were directed toward being offered gigs, opportunities to play their music in front of an audience. If they worked hard and were lucky they might even secure paying gigs, which would allow them to make money by doing what they loved.

The Quarry Men began playing local gigs soon after they regrouped. Most of their jobs during the summer and fall of 1959 were at a youth club called the Casbah, which had recently opened in Liverpool. Teenagers hung out there, talked, and listened to the music that their parents disliked—especially American rock 'n' roll.

Achieving the strong beat of rock 'n' roll was difficult without a drummer, and Lennon had not included one in the new Quarry Men lineup. Drummers were hard to find in those days because most young musicians wanted to be like guitar-playing Elvis. However, Pete Best, the son of the Casbah's owners, liked to play drums, and

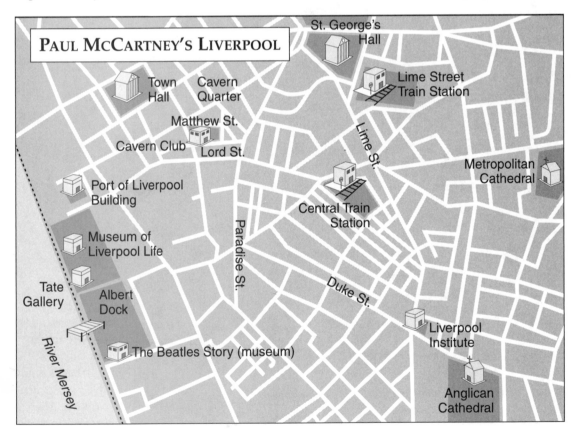

PAUL MCCARTNEY'S LIVERPOOL

St. George's Hall
Town Hall
Cavern Quarter
Matthew St.
Cavern Club
Lord St.
Lime Street Train Station
Port of Liverpool Building
Central Train Station
Lime St.
Metropolitan Cathedral
Museum of Liverpool Life
Paradise St.
Tate Gallery
Albert Dock
Duke St.
The Beatles Story (museum)
Liverpool Institute
River Mersey
Anglican Cathedral

Gang Violence Claims a Beatle

Paul escaped serious injury during the gang fights that broke out at clubs where the Beatles played. Stu Sutcliffe, a founding member of the group, was not so lucky, as biographer Ross Benson explains in Paul McCartney: Behind the Myth:

It was violence without reason and was almost impossible to avoid and one night, in the car park of Litherland Town Hall, it engulfed the Silver Beatles. . . . [During] the show either something was said or one of the gang's girls had taken a fancy to one of the band. Or it may just have been another manifestation of what [Ringo Starr] called the "terrible craziness" of gang ritual which did not consider a night complete until there had been a rumble.

Whichever, a gang of toughs was waiting for the group when they left. The Silver Beatles ran literally for their lives. Stu Sutcliffe didn't run fast enough. He was caught and punched to the ground. And as he lay there the boots went in and he was kicked repeatedly in the head. He would have been stomped to death then and there if Lennon, the one member of the band able to take care of himself physically, hadn't run back and, with fists and feet flailing, dragged him away to safety. But not quickly enough. Two years later, on 10 April 1962, Stu Sutcliffe, the artist who had never wanted to be a rock musician, died of a brain haemorrhage almost certainly brought on by the injuries he sustained that night.

he sat in with the Quarry Men when they performed at the club.

The group also needed a bass guitar player. Lennon had a friend, Stu Sutcliffe, who was a talented visual artist. Sutcliffe had recently sold one of his paintings, which brought him enough money to buy a good bass. He was not a musician and, due to his shyness, had no real desire to be a performer. But Lennon could be very persuasive. In January of 1960, Lennon not only convinced Sutcliffe to use his painting money to buy a bass, he also talked him into joining the group.

Playing the Buckets of Blood

In the spring of 1960, the group, now known as the "Silver Beetles," decided to audition as a backup band for a popular London singer. They failed to get the job, but they did impress Allan Williams, owner of the club where the auditions were held. Williams became the group's agent, and he found the Silver Beetles numerous paying gigs in Liverpool clubs.

As a high-energy form of music, rock 'n' roll demands a reaction from the audience. Most people reacted by dancing. However, in the tough city of Liverpool, violence became a typical reaction to rock music.

The Liverpool gangs that had threatened McCartney as a child were now part of his audience. Violent fights between gangs broke out so frequently at the clubs where rock music was performed that they became known as "blood joints" or "buckets of blood." Biographer Chet Flippo says, "Paul celebrated his eighteenth birthday watching fights from the stage as he played on June 18 at one of the toughest venues around, the Grosvenor Ballroom, . . . where the gang fights were bad to start with and only became worse and worse. The Silver Beetles . . . were quickly learning as much about violence as about music."[35]

After one show, the Silver Beetles were attacked by a gang, and Sutcliffe was beaten severely. During another show, McCartney recalls that a gang member "jumped on stage and grabbed my amp. I think he was going to use it as a weapon. It was only a small one, an Elpico, and I went to get it off him. . . . He said, 'One move and you're dead!'" Paul responded, "'All right, I don't want it then.'"[36]

LEAVING HOME WITH . . .
THE BEATLES

The Silver Beetles played a long series of dangerous gigs in the Liverpool area through the spring and summer of 1960. Then, in August, Allan Williams secured the group a six-week engagement at a club in Hamburg, Germany. McCartney called Pete Best, who had played drums with them at the Casbah, and convinced him to

play with the group full-time so they could accept the gig.

Now Paul had to convince Jim McCartney to let him go to Germany. Paul had just turned eighteen; legally, he could leave home without his father's approval. But he wanted his father's blessing. Jim was worried because he knew that Hamburg was a dangerous city, and he was upset because Paul would need to drop out of school to take the job. Paul used every reason he could think of to sway his father, even pointing out that the Harrisons had given George permission to go and he was only seventeen. In the end, Paul's enthusiasm—and the fact that he would be earning more money than his father—convinced Jim McCartney to let him go.

McCartney, Lennon, Harrison, Sutcliffe, and Best left for Hamburg on August 14. On the way, they decided the group needed a permanent name. All the names they had used—Quarry Men, Johnny and the Moondogs, the Beatles, the Silver Beetles or Beetles, the Silver Beats—were considered. By the time they arrived in Hamburg on August 17, they had pared the list of names down to one: the Beatles.

HAMBURG, BAMBI, AND THE
INDRA CLUB

In Hamburg, the five members of the group were housed in three small, dark, and dirty dressing rooms behind the movie screen of a run-down theater called the Bambi. Their sleeping quarters had no real

John Lennon took this early photo of the Beatles in Amsterdam. From left: Band manager Allan Williams and his wife, singer Lord Woodbine, Stuart Sutcliffe, McCartney, Harrison, and Pete Best.

bathroom; they had to use sinks in the theater's restrooms when they wanted to wash up. And the Bambi was located in one of Hamburg's wildest and most dangerous sections, where drugs, prostitutes, and guns were the main attractions.

Also in this dangerous section was the Indra, where the Beatles performed. The Indra had featured exotic dancers before the group arrived, and many of the customers who wandered in during the Beatle's first few days left when they found out that the dancers were gone. The Beatles had to drum up business by going out to the sidewalk to entice people into the club. McCartney says, "We were always trying to attract people in. This was one of the great learning experiences for us, to attract people who don't really want to see you."[37]

Curious passersby started to come in, and the audience began to grow. This presented another problem for the Beatles: how to entertain a crowd for an entire evening. As Lennon said, "In Liverpool we'd only done one-hour sessions and we just used to do our best numbers, the same ones, at every [show]. In Hamburg we had to play for eight hours, so we really had to find a new way of playing."[38]

That new way of playing included learning new songs. While they practiced new songs, they extended the songs they already knew by playing instrumental sections between verses. McCartney and Lennon learned how to play solos so they could take the lead, sometimes for half an hour at a time, while the other band members rested. Also, they began to improvise during their long solos, creating as many variations as possible on the melodies they knew.

After a few weeks, the band was playing shows that were well attended—and very loud. The Beatles' decibel level became their downfall. Neighbors complained about the noise, and the owner decided to shut down the dance club.

McCartney thought the group would go home once the club closed, but the Beatles' contract required them to play until early October and their time was not up. Also, the contract could be renewed without the group's consent, which meant they could be forced to play for as long as the club owner wanted them. When the Indra closed, the owner transferred the Beatles to one of his more popular clubs, a place called the Kaiserkeller.

MAKING SHOW

The Kaiserkeller had a larger and rougher audience than the Indra, and fights were a common occurrence. Ross Benson, noted McCartney biographer, says, "Hamburg, the gun-running centre of Europe at the time, was a very dangerous city, the Reeperbahn its most dangerous quarter, its waiters employed primarily for their skill with billy clubs and flick-knives . . . and half-dead bodies regularly littered the dance floor." [39]

Long hours and difficult living conditions had drained McCartney's energy by the time the Beatles opened at the Kaiserkeller. He was onstage for six to eight hours every night, with short breaks between sets to catch his breath, change his sweaty clothes, and drink something to soothe his dry throat. In addition, he had to practice before shows, set up and take down equipment, and clean up in the early morning hours after the last set. Even though McCartney loved music, fourteen-hour days made being a musician a very difficult job.

The other Beatles were tired, too, and they all felt threatened by the brutal audience of the Kaiserkeller. These factors made their first shows seem dull, and the owner of the club complained to their agent, Williams, about their lack of enthusiasm. Instead of sympathizing with the Beatles, Williams criticized them, suggesting that they were not working hard enough. He instructed them to move around on the stage more, making a show for the audience to watch. To remind the group of this suggestion, the club's owner began to shout *"mach schau"*—make show—whenever they seemed lifeless. The audience picked up the phrase and shouted it over and over again each night.

The only way the Beatles could quiet the shouting was by giving the crowd what it wanted—wild and crazy shows with as much acting as music. During songs, McCartney and Lennon pranced around the stage, hit each other, shouted insults at the crowd, jumped into the audience, and chased each other around the club. Sutcliffe and Best kept the beat going during these antics. Harrison, who was still the most polished musician of the group, tended to stand quietly on the stage and play his guitar while McCartney, Lennon, and the crowd went into a frenzy around him.

FINDING THE ENERGY TO GO ON

Keeping the Kaiserkeller crowd happy by "making show" forced McCartney to perform as a musician, actor, and athlete, and it left him completely exhausted. The Bea-

tles' contract had been extended through the end of November, so there was no relief in sight.

To find the energy they needed to go on, McCartney and the other Beatles began consuming large amounts of alcohol. The drinking began as a way to please club owners and important patrons. McCartney says:

The club owners would come in late at night. They would send a little tray of schnapps up to the band and say, "You must do this." . . . So you'd [drink] that, because these were the owners. They made a bit of fun of us but we played along and let them because we weren't

---

CRAZY IN HAMBURG

In Yesterday: The Unauthorized Biography of Paul McCartney, *biographer Chet Flippo describes the Beatles' wild antics during their Hamburg performances:*

Sometimes Paul would . . . throw himself at John. Or the two of them would leap from the stage and pretend to be wild bulls rampaging through the dancers. Or John would leap up on Paul's shoulders and the two of them would crash into Stu, knocking him down. Or Paul would butt John from behind while he was singing and the two of them would engage in a mock brawl that would have the lusty Germans cheering.

To their ultimate dismay, the Beatles found that their vituperative "mak show" performances were becoming the hit of Hamburg. The more contempt and anger they displayed—genuine contempt and anger—the more [the club's owner] and the Germans loved it, banging their glasses on the tables and shouting and clapping along. The fans started sending drinks up to the stage for the boys and then began having whole crates of beer and champagne hauled up to them. . . . They began to feel that they could get away with anything onstage and to a certain extent they were right. Fans started referring to them as the "beknakked Beatles"—the crazy Beatles.

great heroes, we needed their protection and this was life or death country. There were gas guns and murderers amongst us, so you weren't messing around here.[40]

The small glasses of schnapps were replaced, over McCartney's next few weeks at the club, with cases of beer and crates of champagne. McCartney and the rest of the band consumed these while on breaks between sets or, when they were too tired to care about their performances, onstage. The alcohol gave McCartney a sense of boundless energy and made him act even crazier during shows.

After a while, even large quantities of alcohol could not keep the Beatles awake and lively during performances. They began taking speed, a drug that increases energy levels and keeps users wide awake, often for days at a time. Many users stop eating regularly, and their bodies become emaciated and unhealthy from the lack of nutrition. Once again, club owners and intimidating patrons were the initial source of the drug and, once again, McCartney felt it would be unwise to refuse their offers.

Home Again

By the time McCartney returned to Liverpool in early December of 1960, the combination of hard work, alcohol, drugs, lack

The band sits onstage at the Cavern Club in Liverpool. On the road, the Beatles indulged in a lifestyle of heavy drinking and drug use.

of food, and sleep deprivation had left him close to a physical breakdown. He was pale and thin. For the first few days after coming home all he did was sleep.

McCartney was not sure what would happen to the Beatles. He had not seen Harrison since the middle of November, when Harrison had been deported from Germany because he was too young, legally, to be in a foreign country on his own. Sutcliffe had stayed in Hamburg with his new German girlfriend, thus informally quitting the group. McCartney and Best had been falsely accused of arson by the club owner, and they had been jailed briefly and then kicked out of Germany.

When Paul regained some of his strength, Jim McCartney suggested that he find an easier job than being a full-time musician. After all, Jim had been happy, as a young man, working during the day and playing music with his band at night. Paul took his father's suggestion. His first job was driving a delivery truck, but he quickly switched to an entry-level job in a factory, where he was encouraged to start working his way up to a management position. Paul was not sure how much time he wanted to spend with the Beatles. "I didn't know if I wanted to go back full time," Paul says. "I quite enjoyed being a working man."[41]

4 Climbing the Ladder to Fame

We were genuinely trying to be artists.

—Paul McCartney

After Paul McCartney and the other Beatles returned to Liverpool at the end of 1960, they were offered only two gigs. Both were at the Casbah, and they were given the jobs primarily because their drummer's family owned the club. McCartney was not concerned. He was busy working at his day job and was still trying to decide if he wanted to be a full-time musician.

The Beatles might have slipped back into their old routine, playing now and then at local clubs, if not for a bit of good luck. On Christmas Day, they heard that the organizer of a big holiday dance needed another band. Although they would share the limelight with other bands, the Beatles took the job.

BUDDING BEATLEMANIA

McCartney had not realized how much he had improved as a musician while in Hamburg until he performed with the Beatles on December 27, 1960. The group had added many new songs to their play list, and those cutting-edge tunes were a hit.

McCartney, Lennon, and Harrison could now play solos, making their performance that night smooth and professional. Instrumental sections between verses kept the crowd dancing and, because some were improvised, made the group's renditions of songs fresh and lively. Most important, the Beatles used their new acting skills to drive the dancers wild. Recalling their performance that evening, Lennon said, "We really came out of our shell and let go. . . . This was when we began to think for the first time that we were quite good."[42]

The audience could not get enough of the group. Teens crowded around the stage, clapping until the Beatles agreed to play more songs. When McCartney tried to climb off the stage at the end of the set, he had to fight his way through hundreds of people.

Before McCartney left the dance hall, the organizer asked the group to play more events and at a higher rate of pay. From January through March of 1961 they received offers to perform almost one hundred shows in clubs, town halls, and ballrooms around Liverpool. Because the Beatles no longer needed an agent to actively seek gigs for them, they decided to drop Allan Williams. Wherever they played, they were a hit. Sam Leach, a rock 'n' roll enthusiast and promoter, remembers one of the Beatles' performances during this period:

> It really was completely magical. . . . They came on, these five figures in black leather, to the opening bars of *The William Tell Overture*. . . . And they were *wild*. Their first number, I remember, was Little Richard's "Tutti Frutti," with Paul on lead vocals. Paul, in particular, used to bomb around stage like a jackknife . . . he got an awful lot of feeling from the kids, and was really *fantastic!* . . . I couldn't believe the dynamism and the charisma.[43]

With so many well-paying gigs lined up, McCartney had no trouble deciding if he wanted to be a full-time Beatle. He quit his day job at once.

Girls scream with excitement as they catch sight of the Beatles. The band's talent and onstage charisma drew thousands of teenage fans to their shows.

TAKING LIVERPOOL BY STORM

In Yesterday: The Unauthorized Biography of Paul McCartney, *Chet Flippo describes Paul's first experience with Beatlemania:*

There were perhaps fifteen hundred dancers on the floor in Litherland that night when the Beatles took the stage and Paul ripped into "Long Tall Sally." All those hours onstage in Hamburg paid off in one hell of a hurry. The musical urgency and authoritative beat these Beatles were laying down, along with their "We don't give a damn" stage presence, was electrifying. The dancers rushed the stage—unheard of at a dance! They swarmed the stage, jumping up and down, yelling, screaming.

Beatlemania struck that night of December 27, 1960. Girls went crazy; guys went nuts. It was a near-riot. The Beatles looked at each other, puzzled. . . . Within two months they were the hottest things going in Liverpool.

HAMBURG (AGAIN) AND THE HOFNER BASS

McCartney and Lennon's ability to put on a show changed the nature of the group's performances. In the past, the group had provided music for events that focused on some other activity, such as dancing. Now, the Beatles were the center of attention. Biographer Chet Flippo notes that "for the first time, their shows were less dances than they were concerts. People came to see them, to watch the band play, rather than to dance and fight and flirt." [44]

Word spread about these well-attended concerts, and in April of 1961 the Beatles' wave of success carried them back to Hamburg. McCartney still had bad memories of that city, but he was excited now because the group would be the center of attention. They would perform at a more

prestigious club this time, sleep in a nicer place, and receive better pay.

However, two issues needed to be resolved before they could accept the job. First, they had to receive permission to return to Germany, where McCartney and Best were not welcome because of their arrests for arson. Sutcliffe and other friends finally convinced German officials to allow McCartney and Best to return, but on one condition. As Sutcliffe wrote in a letter to Best, "One thing they made clear, if you have any trouble with the Police, no matter how small then you've had it forever." [45]

The second problem was finding someone to play bass. Sutcliffe did not want to rejoin the Beatles, and the group's temporary bass player had just quit. McCartney's guitar had recently disintegrated from overuse; he had planned to buy a new instrument anyway. Instead of buying a guitar, he bought a Hofner bass and taught himself how to play.

SINGING THEIR OWN SONGS

Throughout 1961, as the Beatles played night after night in Liverpool and Hamburg, their shows began to set the standard for other bands. Beatle renditions of songs were unique—but only until another group copied them. There was no law against one group copying another: After all, the Beatles were imitating the songs and performance styles of Elvis Presley and other famous musicians.

The need to keep their performances unique sent McCartney and his fellow Beatles on a constant search for new songs. The search was especially important when they played at Liverpool's Cavern Club, where

Liverpool fans line up outside the Cavern Club. In the early 1960s, the Beatles often performed at this popular club.

the best musicians in England not only performed but also picked up ideas from each other. As McCartney recalls, "When we got to the Cavern, we realised everybody and his uncle knew all the tunes we knew, so we started to move towards the B sides [of records] and the more obscure tunes."[46]

To cut down on the time they spent searching for new songs, McCartney suggested they play some of their own. McCartney had begun writing songs when his mother died, and he and Lennon had written many songs together. They had dozens of songs that could be added to the Beatles' play list. "So at the Cavern we started to introduce a couple of our own songs along with these obscure B sides," McCartney says, because the other bands "wouldn't dare do one of our songs."[47]

LENNON-MCCARTNEY, SONGWRITERS LTD.

Some of the Beatles' new songs were written by McCartney, some by Lennon, and some by both, but all were credited to Lennon-McCartney. They chose this designation early in their partnership because Lennon thought the names sounded better in that order. The designation irritated McCartney at the time because Lennon often received praise for McCartney's songs, and it continued to be a major problem for McCartney until 2002, when he released a live album with the order of the names reversed on the songs that he wrote.

Differences between the two men led to many irritations over the years, but they also made McCartney and Lennon an effective songwriting team. When one of them wrote a song that seemed either too superficial or too bitter, for example, the other would add verses that evened out the rough spots. "I could often be a foil to John's hardness," McCartney says. "But it could be the other way round, too. . . . John could be very soft, and I could do the hard stuff."[48]

When they composed, the two men often sat in McCartney's bedroom with their guitars and played with words and tunes

---

THE MAGIC OF SONGWRITING

Paul McCartney describes the magic of composing in Paul McCartney: Many Years From Now, *a biography written by Barry Miles:*

I always liken songwriting to a conjurer pulling a rabbit out of a hat. Now you see it, now you don't. If I now pick up a guitar and start to conjure something out of the air, there's a great magic about it. Where there was nothing, now there is something. Where there was a white sheet of paper, there's a page we can read. Where there was no tune and no lyrics, there's now a song we can sing! That aspect of it made it a lot of fun. We'd be amazed to see what kind of rabbit we'd pulled out that day.

---

until they developed something they liked. Lennon might focus on chords while Mc-Cartney worked on lyrics. Sometimes they worked on different sections of a song and then combined their efforts. The two men spent so much time composing that Mc-Cartney described the activity in terms of an addiction. "Songwriting is a thing we can't stop," McCartney said, "it's a habit, almost."[49]

McCartney and Lennon developed their own composing rules. They could not sit too close when they composed; if they did, their guitars banged together. They must write quickly and do little revising. And when they first composed a song, they could write down the chords but not the words or the melody. As McCartney explains, "if we couldn't remember the song the next day, then it was no good. We assumed if we, who had written it, couldn't remember it, what chance would an ordinary member of the public have of remembering it?"[50]

TAKING ON A MANAGER

McCartney's decision to encourage the group to perform their own songs led to even more success for the Beatles. As Mc-Cartney and Lennon had hoped, the public did remember their songs, and audiences began to request those songs at shows. Also as predicted, other bands did not copy songs written by McCartney and Lennon because it was difficult to learn Beatle songs just by attending shows and because imitating them would be the same as admitting that the Beatles were a better group.

Impressed with the Beatles, Brian Epstein offered to manage the band in 1962.

The Beatles' unique songs kept their performances fresh, and they also increased excitement about the group among Liverpool teens. Soon, people searched for recordings by the Beatles in area music stores, and the group was featured in *Mersey Beat,* a magazine about the local rock scene. The requests and articles made Brian Epstein, a record store manager, curious about the group, and he attended several of their shows at the Cavern Club.

Epstein was impressed by the Beatles, and he asked to be their manager. Jim Mc-Cartney was initially opposed to the idea because he thought a manager might take advantage of Paul, but he gave his consent when Epstein promised to do his best to help the group succeed. Paul and the other Beatles signed a management contract with Epstein and agreed to pay him part of what they earned. "They were fresh and they were honest," Brian Epstein recalled later, "and they had what I thought was a sort of presence and . . . star quality." [51]

"LOVE ME DO" OR NO DEAL

The Beatles took on a manager primarily because he promised to secure them a recording contract. Finding a record company for the Beatles would be difficult for several reasons. Many companies were run by well-to-do Londoners who considered Liverpudlians lower-class people. Also, McCartney insisted that the group be allowed to record their own songs, and few companies wanted to take a chance on composers who were not well-known.

Throughout the early months of 1962, Epstein played tapes of the Beatles for many record companies. He was told guitar-playing groups were no longer the rage and that the group should perform songs by other musicians. After the Decca record company turned down the Beatles, he could not contain his anger. "You must be out of your minds," Epstein told Decca officials. "These boys are going to explode. I am completely confident that one day they will be bigger than Elvis Presley!" [52]

In May, Epstein played several of McCartney's songs for George Martin, an of-

ficial at Parlophone Records. Martin liked the group's sound, but he wanted them to record a song written by an established composer. McCartney refused; he did not want to continue to perform the work of other composers. As McCartney explains, "we wanted our own song. We said we've got to live or die with 'Love Me Do' . . . that's the way we've got to go." [53] His decision to maintain the group's artistic integrity was critical to the Beatles' success.

THE BIG RECORDING BREAK

After serious negotiations with Epstein, Martin agreed to allow the Beatles to record their own songs. However, he would not give the Beatles a contract until they proved themselves in a studio recording session.

In early June of 1962, a few days before McCartney's twentieth birthday, the group entered the Abbey Road studios in London to record several songs, including "Love Me Do" and "P.S. I Love You." "I remember being pretty nervous on most occasions in the recording studio," McCartney says. "It was Us and Them. They had white shirts and ties in the control room, they were grown-ups. . . . [And] then there was us, the tradesmen." [54]

The Beatles received a recording contract, but later the group discovered Epstein had agreed to terms in the contract that cost them millions of dollars. As biographer Ross Benson explains:

It was a contract that would sour Epstein's relations with McCartney in the years ahead, and [it] decisively influenced McCartney's attitude to future financial dealings. . . . In the summer of 1962, however, the Beatles were too inexperienced to bother with the fine print. After all those years of hard work . . . just to have a recording contract was reward enough. [55]

McCartney's Musical Family Comes Together

George Martin wanted the group to record a few more times before they cut a single.

McCartney and the group had two months to polish their performance before the next recording session. As they practiced, McCartney and Lennon realized they needed a drummer with more professional skills than they thought Best had.

In August, Best was asked to leave the group, and the Beatles signed on fellow Liverpudlian Ringo Starr, a friend of Harrison's. The group had met Starr in Hamburg when he was playing drums for another band. With the addition of Starr, the Beatles finally became a stable group, one that provided a source of support for McCartney during the next decade. In years

George Martin sits with a statue of John Lennon on a park bench in Cuba. Martin gave the Beatles their first recording contract.

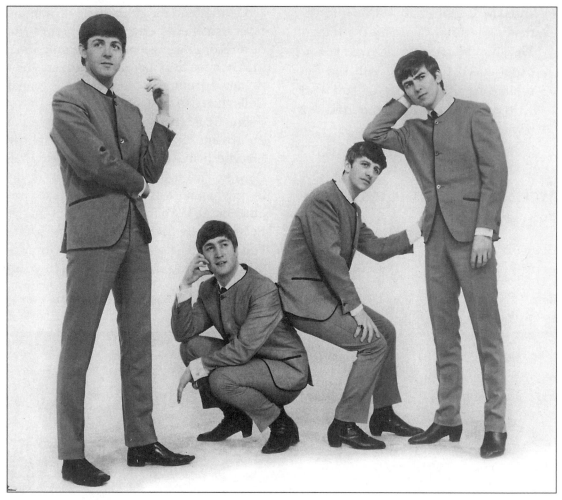

The Beatles pose in matching suits, boots, and haircuts. Manager Brian Epstein suggested that the group adopt this polished, professional image.

to come, each of the men would describe the Beatles as a family. Recently, Starr summed up the feelings of all four men: "They became the closest friends I'd ever had. . . . I felt as though I'd got three brothers."[56]

A BANNER YEAR

After the Beatles recorded "Love Me Do" in September of 1962, they faced several major decisions. The record company wanted to market McCartney as a lead singer and the others as his backup band. McCartney refused out of loyalty to the group. Epstein wanted the Beatles to wear matching designer suits and ties instead of their black leather clothes. McCartney agreed, and he convinced Lennon to accept the new clean-cut image that increased their audience appeal. They were pressured to lose their Liverpool accents, which identified them with the lower classes, but they refused. The accents were a connection to their roots, a connection that became a source of strength and stability when Beatlemania threatened to overwhelm them.

"Love Me Do" was released in October, and by the end of 1962 it was one of the top twenty songs in England. The success of this song always had special meaning for the Beatles. McCartney says, "If you want to know when we *knew* we'd arrived, it was getting into the charts with 'Love Me Do.' That was the one. It gave us somewhere to go." [57]

The success of their first song on the charts ushered in a year full of excitement.

In 1963, McCartney performed with the Beatles in Liverpool and Hamburg clubs and appeared with them on radio and television shows in Europe. Between performances, he maintained a busy recording schedule that led to the release of numerous singles. The group also recorded three albums: *Please Please Me, Introducing the Beatles,* and *With the Beatles.* Several of McCartney's songs, and the songs he cowrote with Lennon, hit number one on the British music charts.

McCartney's trips to the Abbey Road recording studios with the Beatles became so frequent during 1963 that the group decided to rent a London apartment. The apartment seemed fine to the others, but

"GREAT LUCK"

In Paul McCartney: Many Years from Now, *a biography written by Barry Miles, McCartney explains what might have happened to the Beatles if the United Kingdom had not ended its mandatory National Service program, which is similar to the U.S. military draft:*

I don't think there would have been the Beatles. I think we would have been a little group in Liverpool and if we'd been very lucky we'd have had some small success in the local clubs. But then just as we were getting somewhere Ringo and John, being the oldest two, would have had to go into National Service, followed shortly by me and then a year later by George and that would have split any chance of being a group.

I always thought [military service] ruined Elvis. We liked Elvis's freedom as a trucker, as a guy in jeans with swivellin' hips, but didn't like him with the short haircut in the army calling everyone "sir." . . . And I assume that would have been the end for us too. So that was great luck, the government just stopped that [National Service] in time, allowing us the parting of the waves, and we went through and we had the freedom and the sixties.

McCartney recalls that "it was a very cold place. There was no homeliness about it at all. There was nobody's touch. I hated it."[58]

A woman named Jane Asher solved McCartney's housing dilemma. McCartney had met Asher while performing, and they had been dating for several months. Asher was younger than McCartney and still lived with her family in London, although she was already a well-known actress. The Asher family was fond of McCartney, and they invited him to stay at their house. They even gave him a place to practice and write music.

AN INVITATION FROM THE QUEEN

McCartney's fame, and that of the Beatles, grew by leaps and bounds during 1963. Crowds of admirers followed McCartney everywhere. Famous musicians he admired, such as Little Richard and Roy Orbison, invited the Beatles to tour with them. The group performed for the *Sunday Night at the London Palladium* television series, which featured top musical stars from America and England. McCartney and the other Beatles had grown up assuming that, as Starr says, "There was nothing bigger in the world than making it to the Palladium."[59]

However, they soon received an even higher honor. In November, they were invited to perform at a charity concert called the Royal Command Performance, hosted by England's royal family. McCartney says of the event:

> Obviously the main thing about [it] was telling your family, imagining all your parents, uncles and aunties seeing you meet the Queen. . . . [Lennon came] out with the famous line, "Everyone stamp your feet, clap your hands," and then added, "and those of you at the front just rattle your jewelry." We met the Queen afterwards and she was great. We were quite elated because we'd [been received] well and we'd all been so scared.[60]

The level of success McCartney had reached was higher than anything he could have imagined as a struggling musician from a poor family. He was making his living doing something he loved. He had money to attend the theater, the opera, and the openings of art exhibits. Most important, his songs received critical acclaim. By the end of the year, according to music historian Ian MacDonald, the songs of McCartney and of Lennon had become so popular that *The Times* [called] Lennon and McCartney 'the outstanding English composers of 1963.'"[61]

5 Conquering the World with the Beatles

I think we would have been pirates in a different life.

—George Harrison

A hotel room pillow fight early in 1964 celebrated the beginning of a new period in Paul McCartney's life. All of the Beatles were exhausted from performing that day, but McCartney was too excited to sleep. He pounced on Lennon, Harrison, and Starr, pounding them with his pillow and goading them until they fought back. Soon the whole group was laughing, bouncing on their beds, and swinging pillows at each other.

No one could blame McCartney for outbursts of wild exuberance at this point in his career. He was part of the hottest music group in England, and he was one of the country's top composers. A few weeks earlier, the single "I Want to Hold Your Hand" had been released in America. That was encouraging news: British music was seldom released in the United States because it was not well received there. The Beatles' manager had persuaded a reluctant U.S. record company to give the song a chance.

However, McCartney's pillow fight was set off by even better news. "I Want to Hold Your Hand" had just become the number one song in America: The Beatles were about to enter the international music scene.

OFF TO AMERICA

Before the Beatles' first song hit number one in the United States, most Americans had never heard of the group. However,

By the time the Beatles arrived in New York for their first U.S. tour, they were already stars.

McCartney's agent had been so convinced that the group's music would be popular in the United States that he had committed the Beatles to several shows there, scheduled for February.

McCartney worried that the group would not be accepted in America. He had heard that some U.S. disc jockeys played music by the Beatles just so they could make fun of it. Journalists assigned to cover the group had already written scathing articles about the Beatles' odd clothes, effeminate hairdos, and strange music. Frank Sinatra, one of America's top musicians, predicted that the Beatles would bomb in the United States. During the Beatles' plane ride to America, McCartney shared his fears with a fellow passenger: "Since America has always had everything, why should we be over there making money? They've got their own groups. What are we going to give them that they don't already have?"[62]

McCartney's fears dissolved when thousands of screaming teenagers met the group at the New York City airport. More than 250,000 people stood on the sidewalks and cheered as the Beatles drove to their hotel. Murray the K, a disc jockey who became known as the "fifth Beatle" because he spent so much time with the group, kept a live radio broadcast going from their hotel room. Over 73 million people watched the Beatles' first performance on the *Ed Sullivan Show*, more than had ever tuned in to a single show before. When the Beatles performed on the same show a week later, they drew more viewers. By the end of the visit, even Frank Sinatra had to admit that he had been wrong.

A MUTUAL ATTRACTION

The Beatles were successful in America for a number of reasons. Their music was lively. Their look was unique, and they had the mystique of being from a foreign country. They used humor to deal with difficult situations. In addition, McCartney worked hard to develop the group's positive relationships with the public and the press. He became the Beatle who set up interviews, arranged for photo shoots, and went out of his way to meet with fans. Lennon's wife, Cynthia, later remarked that "Paul . . . could have earned his living in public relations."[63]

Also, the Beatles liked the United States, and their genuine enjoyment delighted Americans. McCartney was especially pleased with the warm climate, swimming pools, and motorboats of Miami, where the group spent a few days while taping a second show for Ed Sullivan. McCartney enjoyed meeting famous people in the United States, such as Diana Ross, Don Rickles, and Cassius Clay, the world champion boxer who later changed his name to Muhammad Ali. All the excitement of America could have been overwhelming, but the group's past experiences helped them take it in stride.

The lack of a class system made America particularly appealing to McCartney and the other Beatles. In England, the group's lower-class background would always be an issue for some people. However, in America, where Abraham Lincoln had proven that even a person from a humble background can make it to the top, McCartney's early poverty was an advantage. His life was por-

Ed Sullivan (center) hosted one of the most popular television programs of the 1960s. The Beatles' live performances on his show drew record-setting numbers of viewers.

trayed by the press as a compelling example of what can be achieved through perseverance and hard work.

ONE LONG SCREAM

After the Beatles visited America, the group began a worldwide series of concerts. In every country McCartney visited, crowds of cheering people, held back by fences or police, greeted him. Fans fainted or flung themselves at him when he was whisked by. Touching a Beatle was a goal of many fans, and McCartney, known as the "Cute Beatle," was often the target. Girls climbed onstage during shows or climbed up hotel drainpipes and through his window just to touch him.

And always there was screaming during shows. Audience members, especially female fans, had screamed through some of the Beatles' shows before the group visited America, but now the screaming was constant. The noise could be a blessing, according to McCartney: "People used to say, 'Well, isn't that a drag, 'cause no one listens to your music.' But [sometimes] it was good they didn't because . . . we were playing pretty rough."[64]

HOMETOWN HEROES

The riotous commotion soon followed McCartney to an odd place: his hometown movie theater. Near the end of 1963, a movie company had decided to produce an inexpensive film about the Beatles, just in case they became popular. The Beatles' American visit confirmed their popularity, and filming on *A Hard Day's Night*, which was shot in black and white to save money, began in March of 1964.

McCartney acted in the film, and he and Lennon wrote songs for the soundtrack. They composed in hotel rooms after concerts, in planes on their way to filming locations, in backstage areas before shows, and on movie sets between scenes. The demanding schedule inspired the movie's name and lead song, which is about hard work.

A Hard Day's Night received praise—and excellent box office receipts—when it opened in London in July of 1964. For the first time, a rock group had effectively used the medium of film to entertain both their fans and the people who might never attend a concert. Audiences loved the mock documentary style of the film: while the movie was loosely based on the Beatles'

experiences, it included many elements of fiction. Many believe that *A Hard Day's Night* was a model for all rock films and music videos that followed.

When the Beatles returned to Liverpool for the opening of their movie, more than two hundred thousand townspeople welcomed them back. McCartney says:

> We landed at the airport and found there were crowds everywhere, like a royal [event]. It was incredible, because people were lining the streets that we'd known as children, that we'd taken the bus down, or walked down. We'd been to the cinema with girls down these streets. And here we were now with thousands of people—for us. . . . It was strange because they were our own people, but it was *brilliant*.[65]

STRANGE FAME

As McCartney's fame grew, so did the strange effects of his fame. He first became aware of the effects at a reception for the Beatles held at the British Embassy in Washington, D.C. As journalist Nicholas Schaffner recounts, "The cream of capital society gawked at and mauled the Beatles, in some cases going at them with scissors, intent at snipping off locks of [the group's] famous hair."[66]

Female fans, known as "scruffs," began following McCartney everywhere, and they kept a constant vigil outside the Asher family house, where he still lived. They slept by his front gate or waited for hours in the rain at places where they thought he might appear. McCartney was friendly to the girls, but their constant attention was disconcerting. To avoid detection by fanatical fans, McCartney often left the house by climbing out a window and then sneaking over the roofs of adjoining houses.

The McCartney family home at 20 Forthlin Road became a mecca for Paul's fans, who traveled from around the world to see the place where he grew up. Even though they came at all hours of the day and night, Jim McCartney tried to be polite, often inviting them inside for a visit. The house continued to be a landmark after the Beatles disbanded, and in 1996 it was preserved as an historic site by the National Trust of England.

McCartney also noticed that people assumed he and his band mates were wise

THE BEATLES HAVE LANDED

In The Beatles Forever, *a collection of memories and memorabilia about the group, Nicholas Schaffner shares some of the negative media coverage of Paul McCartney's first visit to America:*

Like a good little news organization, we sent three cameramen out to Kennedy airport today to cover the arrival of a group from England known as the Beatles. However, after surveying the film our men returned with, and the subject of that film, I feel there is absolutely no need to show any of [it].
—Chet Huntley, NBC evening news, February 7, 1964

Having got rich off "teen-age lunacy" in their home [country], these fantastic characters now have come to tap the jackpot— New York, Washington, Miami, American television. . . .

These lads cultivate a vague allusion to being musicians, in a gurgling sort of way. They tote instruments, but blandly assure their fans they know not a note. . . . Their production seems to be a haunting combination of rock 'n' roll, the shimmy, a hungry cat riot, and Fidel Castro on a harangue.
—New York *World Telegram* editorial, February 8, 1964

Visually they are a nightmare: tight, dandified Edwardian beatnik suits and great pudding-bowls of hair. Musically they are a near disaster: guitars and drums slamming out a merciless beat that does away with secondary rhythms, harmony and melody. Their lyrics (punctuated by nutty shouts of yeah, yeah, yeah!) are a catastrophe, a preposterous [mixture] of valentine-card romantic sentiments.
—*Newsweek*, opening paragraph for February 23, 1964, cover story

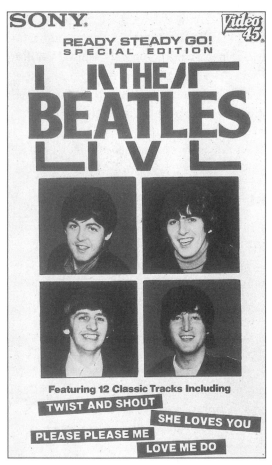

SONY. Video 45

READY STEADY GO!
SPECIAL EDITION

THE BEATLES LIVE

Featuring 12 Classic Tracks Including

TWIST AND SHOUT

SHE LOVES YOU

PLEASE PLEASE ME

LOVE ME DO

This video collection showcases the Beatles' appearances on British television.

simply because they were famous. People asked for his opinion on subjects that had nothing to do with music. He was even asked about the H-bomb, an early weapon of mass destruction. Paul said in 1964:

> We're constantly being asked all sorts of very profound questions. . . . People say, "What do you think of the H-bomb, of religion, of fan worship?" But we didn't really start thinking about these things until people asked us. And even then we didn't get much time to consider them.

What do I think of the H-bomb? Well, . . . I don't agree with it. [67]

GRAB THE LOOT AND RUN

On April 4, 1964, the top five songs in America were by the Beatles, and almost a dozen more Beatle songs were in the top one hundred. Maintaining his emotional balance in the midst of such overwhelming success was a constant challenge for McCartney because, as he says, "You can so easily lose your identity in this sort of business. You confuse the myth with the person you really are. . . . I make sure that being well known doesn't stop me being an ordinary bloke [man]." [68]

The Beatles toured almost continuously from 1964 to 1966, with short breaks to appear on television shows and record their latest songs. McCartney and Lennon composed at a furious pace, turning out extraordinary work under tight time constraints. Acting in *Help!*, another film featuring the Beatles, consumed more of McCartney's time.

In the autumn of 1965, McCartney and the other Beatles took a break to accept Member of the Order of the British Empire (MBE) awards from Queen Elizabeth. The MBE recognizes acts of outstanding courage, charity, and public service on behalf of England. At a traditional ceremony, the Beatles received their awards for service to the arts. It was a great honor, but McCartney had little time to enjoy the event; he had to prepare for his next tour. McCartney's life was like a spinning top, but instead of slowing down, it had started to spin faster and faster.

THE IMPORTANCE OF BEING FUNNY

Irreverent humor set the Beatles apart from other groups and helped them win approval, especially during their first press conference in America, as Nicholas Schaffner explains in this passage from The Beatles Forever:

The reporters who herded into a nearby room . . . knew only that the Beatles were the latest in a long line of teen-age idols, a species that, many could tell from experience, was not noted for sparkling repartée [witty retorts]. But after the stars had made their entrance, and the hubbub of shoving photographers had been quelled, much of the press was disarmed. Whatever the question, at least one of the quartet was always ready with a sharp answer, and, reported a *New York Times* correspondent: "the Beatle wit became contagious. Everyone guffawed. The show was on—and the Beatle boys loved it."

"Will you sing for us?" someone asked.

"We need money first," John Lennon shot back.

"What's your message for American teenagers?"

"Our message is . . . buy some more Beatle records," returned Paul McCartney.

"What about the movement in Detroit to stamp out the Beatles?"

"We're starting a movement to stamp out Detroit."

"Do you hope to take anything home with you?"

"Rockefeller Center."

"What do you think of Beethoven?"

"I love him," said Ringo Starr. "Especially his poems."

"Don't you guys ever get a haircut?"

"I just had one yesterday," retorted George Harrison. Added Ringo: "You should have seen him the day before."

The Beatles play in the Miami surf. The band's antics were popular with fans and journalists.

Gradually, the negative effects of fame began to outweigh the positive effects during tours. McCartney grew tired of the demanding pace. Singing the same songs every day was tedious. The fans' screaming was now a curse, drowning out McCartney's music and making performances seem pointless. The Beatles sometimes just mouthed the words of songs during concerts or, in Lennon's case, shouted obscenities. To become rich, all McCartney had to do was appear at these concerts.

TRYING TO GET A LIFE

Maintaining a personal life in the midst of Beatlemania was difficult. When the group first began their world tours, McCartney was still living with the family of his girlfriend, Jane Asher. The Ashers were kind to him, and they even tolerated the scruffs who camped in front of their house. McCartney enjoyed having a warm and secure place to rest between tours.

Jane Asher was also kind to McCartney, and she tolerated the effects of his fame, including his constant need to be on the road and his desire to maintain relationships with female fans. McCartney thought he might marry Jane, and with this in mind he moved into a large house in London early in 1966. McCartney missed being part of the Asher family, but he liked the independence of having his own place. Jane stayed at the house with McCartney when she was not on tour with a theater company.

In public, they seemed to be the perfect couple, and they became officially engaged.

But they were growing apart, and McCartney's dream of marrying Jane was fading. As McCartney says, "I realised that she and I weren't really going to be the thing we'd always thought we might be. Once or twice we talked about getting married, and plans were afoot but I don't know, something really made me nervous about the whole thing."[69]

FOUR BROTHERS

As McCartney's busy tour schedule continued in 1966, and as he drifted away from Asher, his bonds to the other Beatles grew stronger. The group spent almost all of their time physically close together because, to stay safe, they had to stay inside a tight ring of security. Biographer Ross Benson says, "The limousine lifestyle had been replaced by armoured cars."[70]

Fame gave McCartney enough money to do anything he wanted. However, his sudden fame took away his freedom to do anything on tour except huddle in his hotel room for safety. Beatle historian John Blake says, "The success the Beatles had fought and schemed and speeded for had . . . turned into an anaconda, slowly squeezing all normality and privacy from their lives."[71]

McCartney dealt with the isolation and tedium in a number of ways. He wrote songs with Lennon. Sometimes he joined the group in water fights or ordered unusual items from room service just to see if the hotel would deliver them. Singer Bob Dylan introduced McCartney and the other Beatles to marijuana, and they began smok-

American singer-songwriter Bob Dylan sits at the piano. The folksinger became friends with the Beatles in the mid-1960s.

ing the illegal drug regularly. They could not go out on dates while sequestered, so their road crew brought women to them.

The Beatles were helping to make the 1960s one of the most exciting eras in history. However, McCartney and his band mates were so busy and isolated that they could not enjoy the excitement around them. "It might have been fun for everybody else," Harrison said, "but *we* never saw the Beatles. We're the only people who never got to see us. We were like four relatively sane people in the middle of madness."[72]

DANGEROUS MISUNDERSTANDINGS

The madness had always been dangerous. McCartney and the other Beatles had been knocked to the ground by overzealous fans. They had come close to being electrocuted by faulty equipment. Harrison remembers that, "We almost got killed in a number of situations—planes catching fire, people trying to shoot the plane down, and riots everywhere we went."[73]

In the summer of 1966, the level of danger rose sharply. Imelda Marcos, wife of the leader of the Philippines, invited the Beatles to dinner while they were touring that country. When a misunderstanding kept the group from attending the event, their action

Hairstylists prepare the Beatles for a scene in A Hard Day's Night. *The band's unconventional, shaggy hairdos influenced young male fans to grow their hair long.*

was interpreted as an insult. In response, the group was harassed and threatened, and some members of their road crew were injured, as they made their way to the airport to escape. McCartney says, "We were quite frightened. . . . When we got on the plane, we were all kissing the seats. It was [a] feeling as if we'd found sanctuary."[74]

The danger level rose even higher just before their next tour of America. Once again, the problem was caused by a misunderstanding. Lennon made a remark about the Beatles being more popular than Jesus. Church attendance was declining in many countries, and more people were attending rock concerts; Lennon was simply comparing the two trends. However, many people, including leaders of some U.S. church groups, thought Lennon had meant that the Beatles were more important than Jesus, and a campaign was started to eliminate the Beatles' influence from America.

Ministers preached that the group was evil, the public burned records by the Beatles, and parents forced their sons to cut their Beatle-like long hair. Lennon apologized for his remark in an effort to defuse the anger. As McCartney says, "It was a pretty scary time. John had to apologise, not because of what he'd said, but to save our lives because there were a lot of very heavy [death] threats—not only to him, but to the whole band."[75]

The apology was not as effective as they had hoped. Ku Klux Klan members tried to disrupt their tour. The death threats continued. "By the time we got to the Bible Belt, down South," McCartney says, "there were people banging on our windows. I particularly remember a young boy, maybe eleven or twelve years old, banging on the window of our coach. If he could have got to us, I think he would have killed us."[76]

THE END OF THE ROAD

Tours had brought McCartney more attention as a cultural phenomenon than as a composer. He knew that many serious musicians perceived him as a clown rather than a colleague because of the circus-like atmosphere that surrounded him on the road. Although McCartney would miss the fan feedback tours provided, he began to feel that the other Beatles, who often talked about giving up touring, might be right. He agreed that the group's energy might be better spent on recording.

After the Beatles returned home, safe but shaken, from America, McCartney and his band mates took a long break to think about what they wanted to do next. Harrison went to India. Lennon worked on a film. Starr attended parties. McCartney took a safari in Africa. When they regrouped later in the year, the decision was unanimous: The Beatles would never go on tour again.

Chapter

6 Mantras, Money, Marriage, and McCartney's Mortality

I'm dead, am I? Why does nobody ever tell me anything?

—Paul McCartney

In November 1966, when the Beatles were on break after their last tour, Paul McCartney had an accident. He was driving in the dark when he crashed and was flung from his vehicle. While the accident's details and outcome have sparked heated controversy for years, most people agree McCartney was lucky that night: His injuries seem to have been limited to scrapes, bruises, and a deep cut on his lip.

Confusion about the accident is understandable. If McCartney had gone to a hospital, he would have been recognized, and soon fans would have clogged the corridors and reporters would have tried to snap pictures of the bruised and bloodied Beatle. Apparently, McCartney went instead to the home of someone he knew and had a doctor come there to take care of him. Then he tried to keep details of the crash as dark as the night on which it occurred.

McCartney was fascinated by powerful, random events, and he often incorporated them into his music. An accident that could easily have resulted in death was both random and powerful. It set McCartney's thoughts aglow with ideas about how he could use it in his music.

A New Identity

By the time McCartney crashed, rumors were spreading that the Beatles would not tour again, and music lovers feared that McCartney and his band mates were splitting up. In the middle of November, the group's manager, Brian Epstein, announced that the Beatles were still together. Then he urged the group to release some new songs as quickly as possible to quell the fears of fans.

When McCartney returned to the recording studio, he had grown a mustache to cover the cut on his lip. The mustache changed his appearance dramatically and allowed him to pretend he was someone else. Taking on a new identity, an alter ego, led McCartney to try new things with his music, and as the Beatles planned their next album this theme became a major focus. "I had this idea of giving the Beatles alter egos simply to get a different approach," McCartney says. "It would be a freeing element. I thought we [could] run this philosophy through the whole album: with this alter-ego band, it won't be us making all that sound . . . it'll be this other band."[77]

The resulting work, *Sgt. Pepper's Lonely Hearts Club Band*, has often been called the Beatles' breakthrough album. Although the group had already released over a dozen albums, their hectic tour schedule had restricted McCartney's role in the production to little more than showing up in the studio to record. Freed from the demands of touring, McCartney had time to experiment with his music, using string sections

The Beatles pose with cardboard cutouts of famous people for the cover of Sgt. Pepper. *While making the album, the band experimented with unusual musical styles and recording techniques.*

and wind instruments for backup on some songs. On "A Day in the Life," he secured the services of a symphony orchestra, which he encouraged to improvise. Additionally, he contributed to the development of innovative recording techniques, such as the random cutting and splicing of audio tape segments to achieve unique sounds. He also played a significant role in designing the album's artwork. Biographer Ross Benson says the album

> was the artistic high-point of McCartney's association with the Beatles. It was the moment when everything blended together to produce a work that would establish the group beyond challenge as the most creative musical force of its generation. It expanded the boundaries of pop and sent rock and roll spinning in uncharted directions.[78]

McCartney felt he was also expanding his consciousness while creating *Sgt. Pepper*. At the urging of his band mates, he tried LSD, a powerful hallucinogenic drug. As Paul explains, "I took it with a deliberate purpose in mind: to find the answer to what life is all about."[79]

When *Sgt. Pepper* was released in 1967, people thought many of the songs contained references to LSD and other drugs. This came as a surprise to McCartney, who had written the lyrics. The song "A Day in the Life" referred to drugs but, as McCartney says, "This was the only one . . . written as deliberate provocation to people."[80]

McCartney soon stopped using LSD. However, when he was asked if he had ever taken the drug, he told the truth. The public was angry because they thought the Beatles and their music encouraged young people to take drugs; because of his admission, McCartney became the focus of their wrath.

A MANTRA FROM THE MAHARISHI

Experiencing public anger was one of several events in 1967 that turned McCartney away from the abuse of drugs. In August, Brian Epstein died from an overdose of sleeping pills. Also, Harrison visited San Francisco's Haight-Ashbury district, a section of the city where drug use was common, and brought back horror stories. He had expected to find peace, love, and creativity in people who used consciousness-expanding drugs but, as Harrison said, "It wasn't what I'd thought—spiritual awakenings and being artistic—it was like alcoholism, like any addiction."[81]

Harrison encouraged McCartney and the other Beatles to meet Maharishi Mahesh Yogi, a spiritual leader who taught Eastern philosophy and meditation. McCartney had used LSD to find answers, but he still had many questions. "I think there was a little bit of emptiness in our souls," McCartney says, "a lack of spiritual fulfilment. . . . We were glimpsing bits of bliss and we wanted to know . . . how best to approach that."[82]

In February of 1968, McCartney and the other Beatles flew to India to study meditation with the maharishi. Lennon and Harrison thought they might give up their lives as Beatles and stay in India. McCartney and Starr just wanted to give the spiritual life a try. By April, all of the Beatles had returned to England. The experience had not answered all of McCartney's questions about life, but he had gained valuable training in spiritual practice. He had also gained a mantra, which is a word or series of words that, when chanted during meditation, create a sound believed to help people reach a state of spiritual awakening. The mantra was chosen especially for him by the maharishi, who told McCartney what it was during a simple, private ceremony. As McCartney says, "I always thought I learned what I wanted to learn there. I took it just as a skill like riding a bike. . . . Now I say to my own kids, 'Go and get a mantra.'"[83]

APPLE CORPS

A pressing issue awaited McCartney in England: money. McCartney could have been a millionaire by this point, but his manager

The Maharishi Mahesh Yogi (fourth from left) poses with Lennon, Harrison, McCartney, and other celebrities. McCartney sought spiritual enlightenment from the Indian yogi.

had made bad business deals. Brian Epstein had secured recording contracts that took away McCartney's rights to his music. Epstein had mishandled tour contracts and had made mistakes on merchandizing deals that cost the Beatles millions of dollars. Biographer Ross Benson says McCartney called these deals a "rip off" and that "the financial debacle shaped the rest of his life."[84]

In 1967, McCartney and his band mates had tried to remedy this situation by establishing the Apple Corps to handle their finances. The corporation was like a central bank for the Beatles' money, and they drew funds from it to set up and run companies that ranged from clothing boutiques to electronic research and development groups. Apple Corps was an ambitious project for the Beatles, who had never learned how to manage money. As Peter Brown, their Apple director, said, "They had no way of making the necessary [financial] judgements. We all learn things as we grow up in our transition from school to starting a job. They didn't have that experience. They had either been poor or very rich."[85]

By the time McCartney returned from India, the Apple Corps was out of control,

---

PROVING THEMSELVES TO THE "MEN IN SUITS"

In Yesterday: The Unauthorized Biography of Paul McCartney, *Chet Flippo describes the music industry's class barriers that McCartney worked hard to break down:*

As Paul and John so often talked about later, one of the reasons they were so determined to make it—apart from London's traditional prejudice against "ignorant Northerners"—was the preponderance of rich, stiff-shirted, shallow music-business executives who expected to make lots of money from exploiting "the boys" of the music world. It was a class issue and the Beatles were the first to challenge it. What they faced was a true plantation system. "The boys" were expected to come up with the product, they would be patted on the head, and their product would be harvested and sold by the brilliant executives who owned "the boys." Paul and John were exactly correct in observing that they were originally regarded by the "men in suits" who ran the music business as freaks, as one-shots, as talented idiots who should be milked of whatever quirky gifts they possibly possessed as soon as feasible. "The boys" were not supposed to know what was going on. . . .

In class-ridden Great Britain, for ill-educated, grammar school scouse louts from the North to question anything, that was totally out of the question.

McCartney and American photographer Linda Eastman were immediately attracted to one another. Early in the relationship, Eastman participated in a Beatles recording session.

with many of its companies losing money. To remedy the situation, McCartney took more control of Apple and focused its divisions on things he knew about: records, films, publishing. However, the financial decisions had to be approved by all of the Beatles, who seldom agreed on anything. Business meetings became a chore, arguments were frequent, and cracks began to form behind the flawless façade of Beatledom.

"LOVE IS ALL YOU NEED"

There were cracks in McCartney's personal relationships, too. He and Jane Asher were engaged, but he wanted someone to come home to after work, and Asher wanted to be an actor, not a stay-at-home wife. In July, Asher announced that she and McCartney were no longer engaged.

The previous year, McCartney had met Linda Eastman, an American photographer. They had spent only a few hours together, but their attraction was mutual. Eastman fell in love with McCartney immediately, and she said he later "told me he fell in love with me the first time we met."[86] However, McCartney was still trying to work out his relationship with Asher at that time. He did not see Eastman again until the summer of 1968, when it was clear his relationship with Asher was over. Then he asked Eastman to join him in California for a few days to see if they were still attracted to one another, and they were.

When McCartney returned to London, he asked Eastman to join him. Her daughter, Heather, was starting kindergarten, and Eastman told McCartney—who was used to women rushing to him—that she could not come until her daughter was settled in school. McCartney was touched by this. "Linda was a very good mother," he says. "One of the things that impressed me about her was that she had the woman thing down, she seriously looked after her daughter. . . . She was very kind-hearted too . . . [and] with her I could be completely open." [87]

Eastman came to London a few weeks later, although she wondered how serious McCartney was about their relationship. On September 18, 1968, McCartney gave her an answer: He took her to a recording session and invited her to sing backup for the Beatles on "Birthday," sure signs that McCartney considered her part of the Beatles family.

MARRIAGE, HEARTH, AND A BURNING HOME

In October, McCartney and Eastman spent some time in America so he could get to know Heather. McCartney and Heather became close friends, and McCartney was able to visit places in New York City that he had always wanted to see but had not been able to while on tour. He asked Eastman to marry him, but she suggested that they wait. After a few weeks, all of them returned to London to live as a family. Biog-

rapher Chet Flippo says, "Paul loved it. He wanted hearth and home and animals and kids and earthy smells and mud . . . and Linda cooking up some homemade soup on the stove. It was the perfect home." [88]

It was not so perfect for Eastman. The scruffs who camped outside were extremely jealous and often attacked her when she left the house. Sometimes they came inside when she was gone and stole her things or scribbled obscene graffiti on the walls. Journalists were cruel to Eastman, too, writing negative articles about her clothes, her unshaved legs, and her alleged ability to manipulate McCartney into doing anything she wanted. It took months for McCartney, who was an expert on the subject, to help Eastman handle her new, and somewhat painful, fame.

McCartney convinced Eastman to marry him, and they were wed on March 12, 1969. The scruffs were furious with McCartney for marrying the woman they hated, and they mobbed him, Linda, and little Heather on the day of the wedding. According to Danny Fields, Linda's friend and a rock music expert, "the crowd [became] nasty; kicking, swarming, and actually trying to burn Paul's house down. Police had to come and disperse the angry fans before their little display of jealousy and frustration turned into a riot." [89]

THE SOURING OF APPLE CORPS

Jealousy and frustration were growing inside the Apple Corps, too. Linda's brother specialized in entertainment law, and at the end of 1968 Paul had asked him to help straighten out the corporation's finances. Apple needed help; no one denied that. However, Lennon did not want Paul's brother-in-law taking charge of their finances because he felt that would give Paul too much control. Lennon, Harrison, and Starr chose to work with a different lawyer.

McCartney had already taken on much of the artistic control of the group because Lennon, the unofficial leader, was not able to. His frequent LSD trips left him so weak and disoriented that he had to lie on the studio floor sometimes while the group was recording. However, he did not want to give up his leadership role. Paul says:

> I was trying to get a record made of my song ["Maxwell's Silver Hammer"] the way I wanted it, but I didn't want to offend anyone.... At some point I said, "Look, would you guys tell me what to do?" Then they all went very quiet; we had a day of that, and I remember Ringo coming up and saying, "No, go on. *You* tell *us*. Come on—produce us!" ... It made working conditions pretty difficult and in the end it was getting to be less fun than it was worth.[90]

Throughout 1969, tensions between the Beatles grew. Inside the Apple Corps, the Beatles avoided each other as much as possible. The growing distance between McCartney and Lennon, best friends and soul mates for over a decade, was especially painful. Rock music expert Danny Fields says, "the two halves of one of the century's great songwriting teams, and the engineers who drove the flashiest and most gorgeous locomotive of modern culture, were an unstable entity."[91]

Linda and Paul McCartney pose on their wedding day, with Linda's daughter Heather.

By the fall of 1969, the Beatles' problems were causing stress not only to the group but to everyone associated with them. As Linda recalls, "I was suddenly in the middle of a situation where the Beatles were breaking up, Paul was really upset, there was a whole business and legal thing happening which took everyone's energy and I hated it. I thought [being married to Paul] was going to be all peace and love and music, and it was wartime."[92] To protect himself and his family from the negative effects of the Beatles' disintegration, Paul moved the McCartneys to his farm in Scotland.

BARE FEET, SKULLS, AND A BLACK CARNATION

The McCartney farm is far from highways, towns, and—most important—London. Paul and his family were happy to be out from under the public microscope, and they seldom left the property. To fans and the media, Paul seemed to have vanished.

The McCartney family poses for a photo on Paul's farm in Scotland. Paul moved his family to the secluded farm to shield them from public scrutiny.

At about this time, rumors began spreading that Paul McCartney was dead. Apparently, he had not been completely successful in hiding the events of his November 1966 accident. According to the rumors, that was when he was supposed to have died. Instead of escaping the accident with a cut lip, the buzz was that he had been decapitated. Gossip mongers claimed a man who looked like McCartney had taken his place with the Beatles.

The rumors seemed to explain a lot. The Beatles had stopped touring when McCartney was supposed to have died. And, of course, McCartney's death would be devastating to his band mates, who would make subconscious references to the event in their music.

There seemed to be many references, or clues, in the Beatles' songs and album covers. Several Beatles songs are about driving, death, and violent accidents. Fans thought they heard phrases such as "I buried Paul" and, when they played songs backward, "Paul is dead." Album covers provided many clues: skull-like shadows appear in some cover art; McCartney's picture is often different from those of his band mates; McCartney appears barefoot in several pictures, while all the other Beatles wear shoes; in one case, the other Beatles wear red carnations in their lapels, but McCartney's carnation is black, supposedly symbolizing death.

When McCartney heard the rumors, he responded, "If I'm dead, I'm sure I'd be the last to know."[93] Because of his isolation, this was close to the truth; people around the world had been arguing for weeks about what had really happened to the Cute Beatle. Photographers from *Life* magazine visited Scotland to see if McCartney was alive, and their photo of the McCartneys appeared on the magazine's front cover on November 7, 1969. The photo was supposed to dispel rumors, but many people felt, and some still feel, it did not prove that the real Paul McCartney was alive.

LET IT BE . . . OVER

The "Paul is dead" incident proved the Beatles could not hide important events from the public. Someone was always watching them, and any tidbit of news about a Beatle was valuable.

By the end of 1969, the Beatles had, in effect, died. They could no longer hide their emotional explosions and bickering over Apple Corps and their music, and rumors were leaking out that something serious had happened to the group. There was no official announcement that the group was disbanding because the Beatles still had new music to release, and a breakup would be bad for sales. However, it was clear to McCartney that his life as a member of the greatest rock group in history was over.

7 One Door Closes, Another Opens

Unless something happens, there's nothing to stop Paul and I writing hits when we're old.

—John Lennon

When the Beatles fell apart in 1969, Paul McCartney sank into a deep depression. He had retreated to his farm in Scotland to escape the tensions at Apple Corps. However, he could not escape the feelings of failure and loss he carried with him, and those feelings made him retreat from life. He stopped shaving and washing. He drank heavily. He slept most of the day. "I might get up and stay on the bed a bit and not know where to go, and get back into bed," McCartney recalls. "Then if I did get up, I'd have a drink."[94]

When he was awake, he experienced intensely painful emotional confusion. For years, he had defined himself as a Beatle. Now that his Beatle days were over, he had no idea who he was. Self-doubt overwhelmed him, and he wondered if he would ever be capable of creating music again. "For the first time in my life I was on the scrap heap, in my own eyes," McCartney says. "It was just . . . the terrible disappointment of not being any use to anyone

any more. It was a barrelling, empty feeling that just rolled across my soul."[95]

GOOD FAMILY, GOOD EARTH

Paul's despondence and self-destructive behaviors frightened his wife, and when he began using addictive drugs to dull his emotional pain, Linda knew she had to do something. Fans and journalists had accused her, falsely, of forcing Paul to marry her; recently, they had accused her of forcing him to give up his glamorous life in the city. Now Linda actually did force Paul to do something—give up addictive drugs.

With the help of his wife, Paul shifted his focus away from the death of the Beatles and toward the people and places around him. Being part of a close family had helped him to survive hard times as a child, and having a "family" of band mates had helped him make it through the crazy Beatle years. Now the desire to create a close family for his children—Linda's daughter Heather, whom he adopted, and his first baby, Mary, who was born in 1969—gave him a reason to survive.

Paul had found comfort in nature as a child, and he had been drawn to Linda because she, too, loved the natural world. To help him heal, Linda encouraged him to find that comfort again by exploring the hills and headlands around their farm and

Paul and Linda McCartney watch the sunset on their Scottish farm.

by working in the fields. Journalists were writing mean-spirited articles about what he might be doing in Scotland, but Paul says, "I was just planting trees. I was just getting normal again, and giving myself time to think." [96]

HAVING A GO SOLO

Time to think was essential for McCartney's healing process. But as he began to pull out of depression, his work ethic made him feel he should be accomplishing more. In his fragile state, he found the negative emotional effects of being unemployed overwhelming, especially "a deep kind of emptiness in my soul," McCartney says. "It really made me very frightened.... You sit at home, start boozing and you stop shaving and you *think*." [97]

McCartney had thrown himself into music to deal with his mother's death, but that was back when all of his musical experiences had been positive and when the world of rock 'n' roll was magical and carefree. At this point in his life, music and troubles seemed to go hand in hand. He had become a musician, in part, to avoid taking a regular job, and now making music was the only work he knew.

He needed to work, and, no matter how difficult his experiences with it had been, music was his occupation. To help Paul regain self-confidence, his wife became a cheerleader for his music career. As Linda's friend Danny Fields recalls, she spent hours in 1969 "trying to convince [Paul] that he was a great songwriter.... And so he roused himself from his torpor, renting

UNEMPLOYMENT BLUES

After the breakup of the Beatles, Paul McCartney experienced many of the typical negative emotional effects of being unemployed; he describes a terrifying incident in Paul McCartney: Many Years from Now, *a biography by Barry Miles:*

I was going through a bad time, what I suspect was almost a nervous breakdown. I remember lying awake at nights shaking, which has not happened to me since. One night I'd been asleep and awoke and I couldn't lift my head off the pillow. My head was down in the pillow, I thought . . . if I don't do this I'll suffocate. I remember hardly having the energy to pull myself up, but with a great struggle I pulled my head up and lay on my back and thought, That was a bit near! I just couldn't do anything. I had so much in me that I couldn't express and it was just very nervy times, very very difficult.

small studios or working alone at Abbey Road on his first solo album, *McCartney.* The first song he wrote for it was 'The Lovely Linda.'" [98]

"US AGAINST THE WORLD"

When McCartney released his solo album the following spring, he made the announcement fans had been dreading: The Beatles no longer existed as a musical group. He was still obligated to share with the group any money he earned from his music even if they had taken no part in creating it. Years of legal wrangling lay ahead before he would be free from financial entanglement. But as of April 10, 1970, McCartney had declared his musical independence.

His declaration angered the other Beatles, primarily because they were not ready to make their breakup public. Their anger turned to outrage later in the year when McCartney asked the courts to release him from his financial obligations to the Beatles. Throughout 1971, court actions turned the problems of the Beatles, especially those between McCartney and Lennon, into a public battle. At one point, Lennon is reported to have thrown a brick through the window of McCartney's London house, and several of Lennon's songs from this period include veiled insults about McCartney. McCartney, too, could not resist the urge to make jabs at his ex-partner in lyrics and interviews.

McCartney tried to keep his focus on music. His first solo album received little praise, but it had served its purpose: to prove to McCartney that he was still a musician. His next solo album, *Ram,* hit number one in the United States, but the songs were rough compared to his earlier work. In part, this was because he asked Linda to work with him, and she was just a budding musician. Still, his marriage partner was the only musical partner he had, and, as Paul recalls, "It was very much us against the world at that point."[99]

THE BIRTH OF WINGS

By the middle of 1971, McCartney's veil of depression had lifted and he had regained much of his self-confidence due to his album's success. He felt the urge to perform in public again, something he had always enjoyed. Biographer Chet Flippo says, "Of the four ex-Beatles, he was the one with the real need, almost a physical yearning, to sing before an audience."[100]

Paul wanted Linda to perform with him so they could be together. She was reluctant. Her musical skills were adequate in the recording studio, where songs can be repeated, but she did not feel ready to perform at concerts, where songs had to come out right the first time. Focusing so much of her time on music would make it difficult to continue her work as a photographer. Also, she was in the last months of a pregnancy, and the thought of dealing with three children while on the road was overwhelming. However, Paul finally convinced her to give it a try. "She said, 'If it's gonna be kinda casual and we're not gonna sweat it, we could maybe do something together,'" Paul remembers. "That was the . . . spirit we approached it all in."[101]

Paul's second baby and second band were born within a few weeks of each other. The band came into being in August, when several professional musicians joined Paul and Linda to form a group. The band was still without a name when Linda gave birth to Stella near the middle of September. There were serious complications during Stella's birth, and Paul had to wait outside the delivery room while the doctors worked to save his baby's life. While he waited, he visualized angels hovering around the child to protect her. That image gave him the name of his new band: Wings.

Paul convinced Linda to be a member of his new band, Wings.

ON THE ROAD

As Linda and the baby recovered, Wings rehearsed at the McCartneys' place. This was an era when young people in many countries experimented with communal living, and Paul's farm in Scotland was the ultimate musical commune. The band members lived in various buildings on the property, and Linda cooked meals for everyone. Caring for children, pets, and the farm were as much a part of the band's daily life as guitars and amplifiers.

McCartney had grown tired of the Beatles' performances in big, impersonal venues, where his image, not his music, was the main draw. With his new band, he wanted to play small, informal gigs for

The members of Wings pose while on tour. Paul initially wanted the band to play informal gigs at small venues.

"DON'T KILL US!"

Wings faced many challenges during the recording in Africa of the group's award-winning album, Band on the Run; *biographer John Blake describes two of those challenges—an excruciating bronchial spasm and a mugging—in* All You Needed Was Love: The Beatles After the Beatles:

One day in Lagos while recording his new album, Paul found he could hardly breathe: he gasped desperately for air like a netted fish, before staggering from the fetid atmosphere of the recording studio out into the dusty, noisy African street. Still he could not breathe. It was as though a pillow was being held over his face by some invisible hand. A terrible, searing pain ripped through the right side of his chest and he could feel himself trembling.

"I'm going to die," he thought hazily. . . .

. . . [Another] evening, as he and Linda strolled through a quiet corner of the city . . . a gang of five men began following them in a battered, dusty old car. Paul assumed that, even in this far corner of the earth, he had been recognized. . . . But these men were no curious admirers: they suddenly burst from the car with long-bladed knives—gesticulating frantically—[and] demanded money, cameras, and watches.

"Don't kill us," Linda screamed.

people who wanted to hear his voice. Early in 1972, McCartney packed up Wings, their equipment, the kids, and the family pets for a series of impromptu concerts at colleges and other settings around Europe. McCartney says, "We decided . . . to get in a van and take off up the motorway with a few musicians. . . . Someone would go and say, 'We've got Paul McCartney in the van, do you want him to come in and play?'"[102]

Wings improved by playing for these receptive—and very surprised—audiences. The low-key arrangements—show up and play—allowed McCartney to spend time with his family while he was on the road.

And being paid for performing made him feel, finally, that he was employed again. To critics who complained that his new songs were not like the songs he had created with the Beatles in the 1960s, McCartney responded, "It may not be the Sixties, but nothing's the Sixties anymore except the history books. It's the Seventies and it's hip and it's happening."[103]

FUGITIVE BAND

The first Wings album was poorly received, and the second was successful but not as powerful as McCartney would have liked.

For the third album, McCartney tried a trick he had learned with the Beatles. The concept of adopting new identities had made the Beatles' *Sgt. Pepper* album cohesive and exciting. He would make the next Wings album cohesive by using the concept of a band escaping from something. For *Sgt. Pepper*, the group had changed their appearance. For the new Wings album, *Band on the Run*, the group would change their location.

The album was recorded in 1973, primarily in Nigeria, and many random events that happened during its creation seemed to fit the album's concept. Two band members quit just before Wings flew to Nigeria, leaving only three "survivors" and adding a life-on-the-edge quality to the project. They arrived in the monsoon season and were troubled by mud and bugs. The recording studio was not ready, so the group had to be inventive and make do with what they had. At one point, the band members were mugged and the recording session tapes were stolen.

All of these events led to a high-energy album that brought McCartney praise from critics and the public—and that bolstered the sagging McCartney family bank account. Even Lennon, who had criticized all of McCartney's post-Beatles music up to this point, praised the album. Harrison also paid McCartney and his new group a compliment when he said, "If you want the Beatles, go see Wings."[104]

ROCKING ON THE WATER

Now that critics and the public liked Wings, Paul decided it was time to do a world tour, and he scheduled one for 1975–1976. Linda was terrified of performing for thousands of people. The critics and the press were ready to pounce on her for any mistake, and fans often made fun of her singing. Journalist Jeff Giles says Linda wanted to leave the band, but "Paul, who can be epically willful, wanted her to stay. She stayed."[105]

The tour, *Wings over the World*, set world records for attendance, surpassing those set by the Beatles. The tour also resulted in another hit album. Paul was pleased with the success of the tour, but he was even happier that Linda had overcome her fears. However, he admitted later that pressuring her to do the tour was unfair and had caused them problems.

In 1977, buoyed by the success of their last album, Paul decided Wings would record in another exotic location—on boats anchored near the Virgin Islands. Paul and Linda dealt with several problems: Custom officials conducted drug inspections; park rangers asked them to stop singing after 10:00 P.M.; and band and crew members experienced infections, sunstroke, electrocution, and partial deafness. On top of all this, Linda was pregnant; their fourth child, James, was born in September. Acknowledging the challenges they faced during this and their other adventures together, Paul says of their marriage, "You get this picture of us swanning along in a little rowboat managing to avoid the white water, but we were right in the middle of that white water, man, so it's even more miraculous that we made it."[106]

Paul says they made it because Linda was the anchor that kept him steady in the

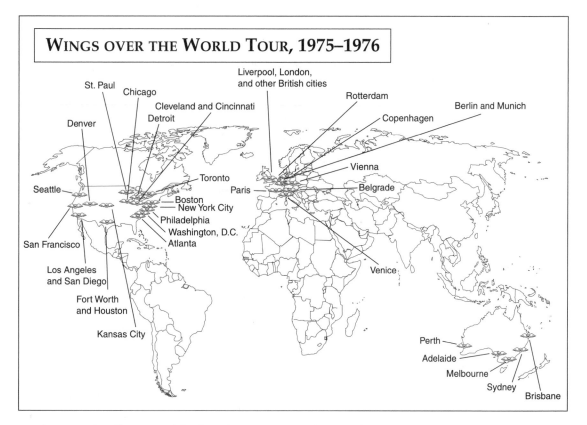

WINGS OVER THE WORLD TOUR, 1975–1976

pitching and rolling world of rock music. She cared for their children, the farm, and Paul during his period of depression. She was, because of her years of experience as a photographer, a compatible and knowledgeable artistic partner with whom Paul could share creative ideas. She even became a performer because, as Paul admits, he needed her onstage with him to bolster his confidence.

FLYING HIGH

By the fall of 1979, a decade had passed since the beginning of McCartney's painful post-Beatle depression. He had risen steadily from that low point, putting together a band that rivaled the success of the Beatles, performing for large concerts around the world, winning many awards, and achieving fame once again. He had released "Mull of Kintyre," a song that became the best-selling single ever in Britain. In October of 1979, according to biographer Geoffrey Giuliano, McCartney was "honored by the Guinness Book of World Records . . . [and] presented with a valuable rhodium disc for being the most successful songwriter in the history of popular music."[107]

The famous attract attention: Paul had learned that lesson well over the years. However, he had also learned that the only way to stay sane was to go about his life as if he were not under constant scrutiny. He did what he wanted, and one thing he

WASHED UP

Paul's arrest in Japan for possession of marijuana was traumatic, but he relied on music and humor to help him survive while in prison, as Geoffrey Giuliano explains in Blackbird: The Life and Times of Paul McCartney:

Washing with the water from his latrine [toilet] was understandably getting [McCartney] down. After a week of this he humbly asked if he might be allowed a bath, a proposition passed along through the incredible Japanese bureaucracy as if they had been faced with a constitutional amendment. . . . [The] request was finally granted and Paul was led into the communal bath house, much to the amazement of the other prisoners. "Alright, lads," said McCartney, instantly "on" as he always is whenever confronted by a crowd. "How are ya?"

Stripped naked virtually in front of everyone (by now even the off-duty guards had gathered to observe the spectacle), McCartney made the most of the situation. Eyes twinkling, head cocked, and arms outstretched, the incurable showman belted out the first few lines of "Mull of Kintyre" and, instantaneously, everyone joined in. As the Japanese voices rose in pitch even the assembled fans keeping vigil outside the jail began to sing. From the little boy who started singing and playing guitar in the bathtub so many years ago back in Liverpool, McCartney had now come full circle, prompting Jo Jo Laine [wife of a Wings member] to quip, "Paul has played some of the classiest restrooms on the planet."

wanted to do was to smoke marijuana with his wife. During his Beatles days, the police had overlooked his use of illegal drugs. But times had changed, and Paul and Linda had been arrested several times in the 1970s for possessing marijuana. After one incident, Paul said: "At the end of the day most people go home and have a whiskey. . . . Well, we play a gig and we're exhausted, and Linda and I prefer to put our kids to bed, sit down together and smoke [marijuana]," and "we're not changing our lives for anyone." [108]

Soon after McCartney received his Guinness award, Wings began what was to be an extensive world tour. In January of 1980, near the beginning of the tour, McCartney arrived at Japan's Narita International Airport with Wings. He also arrived with marijuana in his suitcase. The drug was discovered at the airport, and McCartney was immediately handcuffed, arrested, and taken to jail.

FALLING HARD

Being incarcerated in a foreign country was terrifying for McCartney. He was kept in a dark cell. He could not communicate clearly with the unsympathetic guards. He had heard he could receive a prison sentence of seven to ten years for his offense. To keep himself from sinking into despair, he sang. Even though most of the prisoners on his cell block did not understand English, they knew some songs by Paul McCartney and the Beatles, and they sang along.

Linda was terrified, too. After Paul's arrest, she took their children to a hotel and waited for some word of what had happened to her husband. Linda said of the incident, "I was so frightened for Paul I can't even describe it. . . . Your imagination takes off. I didn't know what they would be doing to him."[109]

After nine days in jail, Paul was released, and the McCartneys flew home. The Wings world tour was canceled; even if concert dates could have been rescheduled, McCartney was too traumatized by his incarceration to go onstage. Also, his Wings band mates were upset with him because his thoughtless action—possession of an illegal drug—had cost them their tour pay. Tensions developed. Although Wings did not officially disband until 1981, the group unofficially dissolved soon after McCartney's arrest.

"UNLESS SOMETHING HAPPENS"

For McCartney, 1980 had a disastrous beginning due to his arrest. The year had an even more traumatic ending. On December 8, a man whose obsession with the Beatles had reached the point of insanity shot and killed John Lennon in New York City.

Distraught fans gather outside John Lennon's New York City apartment after his murder. McCartney was shocked by Lennon's death.

The next day, reporters crowded around McCartney and stuck microphones in his face, eager to get his response to the murder of the man who had been his best friend for years. McCartney had always been the Beatle most willing to meet with reporters, but he had never had to discuss something as horrifying as murder, and the words he mumbled to the reporters that day made no sense. He still had trouble speaking about Lennon's death several years later when he was asked, in an interview, how he had felt when he found out that Lennon had been murdered. "It was crazy," McCartney said. "It was anger. It was fear. It was madness. It was the world coming to an end." [110]

In addition to feeling shocked at Lennon's death, the surviving Beatles wondered if they were targets, too. To keep his family safe, Paul improved the security around his home and hired full-time guards. The other Beatles took similar precautions. The efforts were not completely successful: Linda was nearly kidnapped at one point, and, years later, an intruder attacked and wounded Harrison in his home.

After McCartney emerged from his state of shock, he was grateful that he and Lennon had made efforts to overcome their past differences before Lennon died. By the end of Lennon's life, they had visited each other several times, even playing music together on a few occasions. During their visits, they talked about simple things—marriage, children, cooking. And they felt that the wounds they had inflicted on each other were beginning to heal.

In the years since Lennon's death, McCartney has found comfort in a conversation he had with Lennon when they were young. They were talking about what would happen after they died, and McCartney recalls that Lennon was worried about how people would remember him. To this McCartney responded, "You'll be remembered as something fantastic." [111]

Chapter

8 Spreading His Wings

My whole thing over the years has been . . . one giant experiment.

—Paul McCartney

As a teen, Paul McCartney dreamed of having enough money to buy a fast car, a decent house, and a fine guitar. Biographer Ross Benson says McCartney's "declared ambition, according to the first official Beatle handout, . . . was to make a lot of money. After he'd done that, he said, he wanted to retire."[112]

By the early 1980s, McCartney's dream had become reality. He was rich, with enough income from royalties to maintain his wealth even if he never sang another song. After all his recent troubles—his arrest, John Lennon's murder, the end of Wings—it would have been understandable if he had chosen to retire.

McCartney kept working. He was facing his fortieth birthday, a milestone that was a wake-up call for him. There were many things he still wanted to do and a limited number of years left in which to do them. McCartney says he continued to work because "there's an urge . . . to stop the terrible fleetingness of time."[113]

An intense focus on his career for a quarter of a century had helped McCartney climb to the top of the popular music ladder with the Beatles and with Wings. Now he stood on the top rung of success and wondered where he should go from there.

FACING THE WHITE CANVAS

McCartney was labeled a popular musician, but he wanted to be more than that. He wanted to develop new interests and to work on projects he had found appealing over the years but had been too busy to pursue. At age forty, McCartney finally took the time to explore other modes of creative expression, and he began by focusing on painting.

McCartney had always enjoyed visiting art galleries, and he had helped design album covers. However, he needed a catalyst to change his appreciation of art into a passion for creating it. That catalyst was Willem de Kooning, a painter who invited McCartney to visit his studio. Watching de Kooning paint inspired McCartney to buy art materials—charcoal pencils, oil paints, canvasses—and experiment with them.

McCartney was more interested in the process than in the final product. He wanted to enjoy the act of spreading paint

McCartney stands between two of his abstract paintings. In recent years, McCartney has gained critical respect as a visual artist.

on canvas, to use painting as a way to relieve the stress of his music career. For these reasons, McCartney adopted a low-key approach, which he describes as "just to have a go with paint, to play with it."[114]

The low-key approach made McCartney hesitant about showing his work to the public. An exhibit might prompt criticism, which could destroy his enjoyment of painting. When he finally agreed to a small show, he was surprised to find that both the public and the art critics liked his abstract paintings, which he gave whimsical names such as *Brains on Fire, David Bowie Spewing,* and *A Greener Queen.*

Praise for his work was so strong that the exhibit led to the publication of a book of his paintings and then to his creation of a series of abstract images for postage stamps. In 2002, a major exhibit of his work was held at the prestigious Walker Gallery in Liverpool. Critical acclaim for the show proved that, after twenty years of having "a go with paint," McCartney had established his reputation as a serious painter.

More Creative Crossovers

His successful crossover into visual art encouraged McCartney to try other art forms. He began writing poetry, a natural extension of his work as a lyricist. Although lyrics and poems are similar, McCartney's challenge was to discover their differences so he could create poems that did not need music to make them powerful. Critic Adrian Mitchell says that McCartney, whose first book-length collection of poems was published in 2001, was successful and has become "a jeweller and a juggler when it comes to words."[115]

McCartney used his music, visual art, and writing skills when he turned his attention to filmmaking. He had shot experimental film clips in the early 1960s and had gained a deeper appreciation for film-making while starring in several movies about the Beatles. However, he had never set aside the time to do serious film work until this period in his life.

McCartney's first full-length feature film, *Give My Regards to Broad Street*, opened in 1984. He wrote, directed, produced, created the soundtrack for, and performed in the movie, which is loosely based on his life as a rock star but includes fictional elements that make it a fantasy adventure. Although the movie received mixed reviews, the response encouraged McCartney to keep working on films.

An animated short, which McCartney created to accompany his feature film, received better reviews. The short is about Rupert the Bear, his favorite storybook character as a child, and the British Academy of

MAGICAL DISTORTION

In Paul McCartney: Many Years from Now, *a biography by Barry Miles, McCartney describes the creative process of distortion that he uses in music and in other art forms:*

With everything, with any kind of thing, my aim seems to be to distort it. Distort it from what we know it as, even with music and visual things, and to change it from what it is to what it could be. To see the potential in it all. To take a note and wreck it and see in that note what else there is in it, that a simple act like distorting it has caused. To take a film and superimpose on top of it so you can't quite tell what it is any more, it's all trying to create magic, it's all trying to make things happen so that you don't know why they've happened. I'd like a lot more things to happen like they did when you were kids, when you didn't know how the conjuror did it, and were happy to just sit there and say, "Well, it's magic!"

Film and Television Arts (BAFTA) voted it the best short animated film of the year. *Daumier's Law,* an animated short about the work of Honoré Daumier, a French artist who lived in the 1800s, brought McCartney another award from the BAFTA. *Tuesday,* his fantasy movie about frogs, was featured at the Venice Film Festival.

Perhaps McCartney's most innovative film project so far is *The Grateful Dead—A Photofilm,* a documentary-style tribute to the popular rock group. Although it is a movie, the images used to create it came from a series of Linda McCartney's still photographs of the Grateful Dead. Using digital imaging techniques, McCartney made multiple copies of the photographs, each slightly different from the others, then filmed the copies one after another to create the illusion of movement. This is the same technique used in "flip books," in which objects appear to move when the book pages are quickly flipped through.

McCartney finds that the general approach he used for music works well for all of his creative projects. "You learn that it is good to be spontaneous, it is good to be thorough, it is good to have something that inspires you, it is good to be in a great mood, and all these things cross over," McCartney says. "And this idea of not worrying too much. If an idea doesn't come, you can just go for a walk, you know, not be too intense."[116]

SOLOS AND DUOS

McCartney's first love was still music, but he was not anxious to join another rock band immediately after Wings broke up. He wanted to try something different with his music. Also, he wanted to maintain absolute artistic control over his work, which is hard to do as one member of a band with several voting members.

His brief stint as a solo artist after the Beatles broke up had pleased McCartney, and he returned to the solo format in the 1980s. Solo work had an important advantage: It gave him complete freedom over his music. However, the format also had a major drawback: Working on his own left McCartney longing for the excitement that can happen when musicians collaborate and share ideas.

To fill his need for musical mates, McCartney sought out other world-class musicians—Stevie Wonder, Michael Jackson, and Elvis Costello—and worked with them as performing or songwriting teams. Although these relationships were not as close as the one McCartney had had with Lennon, all resulted in award-winning songs or albums, such as "Ebony and Ivory," "Say, Say, Say," and *Flowers in the Dirt.*

Over the years, McCartney has been involved in three induction ceremonies at the Rock and Roll Hall of Fame. He was inducted as a member of the Beatles in 1988, although he did not attend the ceremony. He gave the acceptance speech for John Lennon, who was honored posthumously as a solo artist in 1994, the first person ever to be inducted twice. And in 1999, in recognition of the rock music he created during his post-Beatles period and after the breakup of Wings, McCartney was inducted as a solo artist into the Rock and Roll Hall of Fame.

In the early 1980s, McCartney recorded a hit song with Michael Jackson. He also worked with Stevie Wonder and Elvis Costello.

CLASSICAL KUDOS

McCartney was on familiar ground with rock music, but his next musical experiment sent him on a journey into unexplored musical territory. In the late 1980s, he decided to create music in the classical style. McCartney was as surprised by this decision as anyone. His family had never liked classical music, and McCartney had thought it was, like painting, something he could only appreciate from a distance. Also, the piece he had in mind, an oratorio, would be over an hour and a half in length, much longer than any music he had created before. To explain the difference in length, McCartney describes the typical rock song as a poem and the oratorio as a novel.

Working on the oratorio was a long process of experimentation. McCartney put together different musical elements to see what would happen, using what he calls the random principle. It is an imprecise process, but one that results, McCartney believes, in high-energy art. "One thing I have learned, not just about painting, but in life in general," McCartney says, "is that the more precise you try to be about a thing, somehow the less you achieve. You can . . . lose the spirit of the thing."[117]

BACK ON THE RUN

At the same time McCartney was creating the oratorio, he decided to tour again. His break from touring, which he decided to extend for safety reasons after Lennon was murdered, had kept McCartney off the road for nearly a decade. Although he was still concerned about safety, he missed the excitement of performing for audiences.

He chose to return to the rock band format for the tour. However, he had no intention of giving up control over his music. To ensure that he would make all final decisions, McCartney put together a backup band and formally established his position as the leader. Linda, once again, was included in the group so his family could be together while on the road.

McCartney played over one hundred concerts during his ten-month world tour, which began in 1989. His performances in cities around the world attracted bigger crowds than those of many younger musicians. Over 180,000 people came to listen to McCartney at a stadium in Brazil, the largest group ever to attend such a concert. McCartney was grateful for the support of his fans, who had not forgotten him and had made his first tour in a decade a success.

STAYING ALIVE

One of McCartney's most important accomplishments might seem like the simplest: to stay alive in the world of rock music. McCartney biographer Ross Benson says McCartney's ability to survive "amongst the burnt-out carcasses that litter the foot-stomping, mind-blowing world of rock

McCartney holds a copy of his Liverpool Oratorio, *the first major classical piece he ever composed.*

Recording classical music was a major challenge for McCartney because he could not—and still cannot—read music. He had to hum different parts of the composition, or pick out phrases on the piano, so musicians could then convert the sounds into written notes. It was a tedious process, but McCartney was willing to work hard, and the result was gratifying. His *Liverpool Oratorio* surprised fans and critics alike, and it hit the number one spot on Britain's classical music charts.

and roll, is its own remarkable achievement."[118]

While many factors, including good luck, have contributed to McCartney's survival, perhaps his most valuable asset has been his curiosity. He decided early in life that he wanted to learn about many subjects, and achieving this goal has given him a reason to keep going. As McCartney said at age twenty-four, "I'm trying to cram everything in, all the things that I've missed. People are saying things and painting things and composing things that are great, and I must know what people are doing."[119]

His active curiosity has made him eager to try the technological innovations that have allowed him to change with the times. As a Beatle, he was one of the first musicians to use films to replace tours. Today, he uses television specials, live webcasts, a website, and on-line chats to communicate with fans. When he needed a break from rock bands, his curiosity about painting, writing, filmmaking, and other musical styles and formats kept him from resting on the cushion of his past success.

SHOWING HIS GRATITUDE

Critics had often called the Beatles ungrateful because they did not seem to use their money to help others. The group had tried to set up the Apple Corps to support social causes and the arts, but their efforts were mostly ineffective due to the group's lack of financial experience. McCartney was often the focus of this criticism. Growing up in a poor family had taught him to be careful with money, and this was some-

times interpreted as stinginess. The interpretation was not accurate; he could be very generous. However, because most of McCartney's donations were anonymous, they went unnoticed.

The myth that he was a miser grew during the years when Beatle legal battles tied up much of his income. When he regained control over his finances, McCartney was determined to use his money to make a

Paul and second wife, Heather Mills McCartney, support many charitable causes.

positive difference in the world. He began by supporting the arts, which had been his avenue to success. In the early 1990s, he helped found the Liverpool Institute for the Performing Arts (LIPA). LIPA is a school that trains dancers, musicians, actors, and other students interested in the entertainment business. Knowing that his name would encourage other patrons to support the school, McCartney made public this act of generosity. To the students' delight, McCartney also donates his time, stopping by the school occasionally to lead seminars.

The school is located in the old Liverpool Institute building, where McCartney attended classes as a child. The school building was scheduled for demolition when he was making plans for LIPA, and McCartney saw a way to make his money serve two purposes at once. By renovating the building and then housing LIPA there, he not only founded an arts academy, he also preserved a historic architectural treasure. McCartney's founding of LIPA, which serves the needs of artistic young people from around the world, was a key factor in his selection in 1997 for knighthood, an honor that gave him the new title of Sir Paul.

STRAIGHT FROM HIS HEART

McCartney's charitable work was often influenced by Linda, and she encouraged him to support social and environmental causes. The list of causes Paul and Linda supported is long and diverse: anti–fox hunting, vegetarianism, the environmental group Friends of the Earth, the human rights group Amnesty International, and the animal rights group PETA, for example. However, a common thread connects the causes. Paul pointed out the connection when he was asked what one thing he would like to change about the world. He said his main concern was stopping violence—to animals, to humans, and to the environment.

In the mid-1990s, Linda's health influenced Paul's decision to support another cause. The McCartneys were devastated, at that time, when Linda was diagnosed with breast cancer. When her cancer spread and threatened to take her life, Paul faced a major challenge. To survive the pain of his mother's passing, he had learned to hide his feelings. This made coping with death very difficult for him. Paul's discomfort had caused him to blurt out comments that seemed uncaring when his mother died and then again when Lennon was murdered. During Jim McCartney's last days in 1976, when the elder McCartney was suffering from bronchial pneumonia, Paul stayed away because he could not bear to see his father die. Now Linda needed him. To be a rock of support for her, as she had always been for him, he would need to deal with painful feelings.

Paul met the challenge well. He encouraged Linda during her cancer treatments. He cared for her after the treatments failed. He comforted her during her last moments of life, holding her hand while she faded away. As she was dying, Paul reminded her of the fields and woods of the ranch they often visited in Tucson, where

SPEAKING FOR THE ENVIRONMENT

In Paul McCartney: I Saw Him Standing There, *Jorie Gracen's collection of McCartney tour photographs, essays, and interviews, McCartney talks about using his fame to support environmental and animal rights causes:*

The way I look at it is, in many ways, we're the voice of the people I meet. The people I meet will talk about this and be very interested, obviously, in saving the planet—many of them in protecting animal rights. But no one is going to listen to them. They can't command these press conferences. So, rather than just use [press conferences] to talk about me, a record, or the gigs, I do like to try and introduce other issues that are important to me. . . .

Sometimes I would cite John's writing—"Give Peace a Chance," for instance—at the end of the Vietnam War. When you see the film of what is near a million people, singing that song to Nixon at the White House, I'm sure it [had] some effect. . . . So, I think whilst environmental things can't just be cleaned up instantly, 'cause they are expensive, I'd like to try and direct people's thinking and focus it toward that. If they think I'm just doing it for my own career, well I say, "Look, you sort it out. You get the governments to sort it out and I'll sit down. You clean up these oil spills. You close that hole in the sky. I promise I won't say anymore. But till then . . . I'm a father of four kids, you know. I want to see this place get sorted."

she loved to take long walks. He told her stories about her favorite horse. After Linda died, Paul recalls feeling such intense pain that he thought his heart might break.

Now, in addition to the other causes Paul McCartney supports, he also makes donations to cancer research centers and hospitals to honor the people close to him who have died from this illness—his mother, his wife, and his fellow Beatle George Harrison, who died in 2001. At McCartney's recent art exhibit in Liverpool, the curator, noting the depth of feeling in McCartney's paintings, music, and efforts to help others over the years, observed that all of McCartney's work has come straight from his heart.

IN HIS SIXTIES

As a teen, McCartney wrote a song in which he wondered if he would still be loved and needed when he reached his sixties. McCartney has reached that point in his life now. His fans still need him. Also, he has the love of Heather Mills, a woman he met while working on human rights causes; they were married at a castle in Ireland in 2002. The evidence is in, and the answer to the question McCartney asked so many years ago—"Will you still need me?"—is indisputable: yes.

By continuing to develop as a musician, visual artist, and filmmaker, and to produce work that competes on an equal footing with the work of young people,

Paul McCartney overcame childhood poverty, tragic loss, and the pressures of international celebrity to become one of the world's most esteemed artists and humanitarians.

McCartney has proven it is possible to be a successful artist at any age. He has also proven that success and a career in the arts are within the reach of everyone. Over the decades, he has kept his skills sharp and his curiosity alive. For all these reasons, journalist Andrew Walker calls Paul McCartney "a modern-day Renaissance Man."[120]

"KEEP ON ROCKING"

At the end of the twentieth century, the BBC asked its audience to vote for the best composer of the past millennium. The top ten choices included a wide range of musicians, from Beethoven, Bach, and Mozart to John Lennon, Bob Dylan, and Prince. Paul McCartney was number one. His position at the top of the list brought him another title: "the greatest composer of the last thousand years."

McCartney's recent frenzy of activity, including an extensive rock tour of the United States, guarantees that his musical influence will extend well into the twenty-first century. He still refuses to retire. Even if no one comes to his shows, McCartney insists he will perform music as a hobby, driven by a powerful force to simply "keep on rocking."[121]

Songwriter, rock musician, solo artist, performer of duets, bandleader, and classical composer: Paul McCartney has spent a lifetime exploring all areas of the musical terrain. When asked what he will do next, McCartney says he's not sure, "but I know it's going to be interesting, a fascinating voyage."[122]

Notes

Introduction: A Good Knight in the Kingdom of Rock

1. Quoted in Timothy Tilghman, "Celebrating Freedom on a Global Scale: Paul McCartney Kicks Off Super Bowl XXXVI," *Rock on Tour*, February 2002. www.rockontour.net.

2. Quoted in Paul Kennedy, "Tower's Heroes Reminded Me of Dad, Says Paul," *Liverpool Echo*, September 28, 2001. http://icliverpool.ic network.co.uk.

3. Quoted in Laura Tuchman, Jan Herman, and Michael Ross (plus wire reports), "Star-Studded Show Staged as Tribute to Sept. 11 Heroes," *MSNBC.com*, October 21, 2001. www. msnbc.com.

4. Beatles, *The Beatles Anthology*. San Francisco: Chronicle Books, 2000, p. 356.

5. Chet Flippo, *Yesterday: The Unauthorized Biography of Paul McCartney*. New York: Doubleday, 1988, p. 372.

6. Quoted in Barry Miles, *Paul McCartney: Many Years from Now*. New York: Henry Holt, 1997, p. 617.

Chapter 1: Frontier Childhood in War-Torn England

7. Ross Benson, *Paul McCartney: Behind the Myth*. London: Gollancz, 1992, p. 13.

8. Beatles, *The Beatles Anthology*, p. 17.

9. Quoted in Miles, *Paul McCartney*, p. 6.

10. Beatles, *The Beatles Anthology*, p. 17 .

11. Paul McCartney, *Paintings*. Boston: Little, Brown, 2000, p. 43.

12. Quoted in Miles, *Paul McCartney*, pp. 7–8.

13. Quoted in Chris Salewicz, *McCartney: The Definitive Biography*. New York: St. Martin's, 1986, p. 29.

14. Quoted in Miles, *Paul McCartney*, p. 10.

15. Quoted in Miles, *Paul McCartney*, p. 10.

16. Quoted in Miles, *Paul McCartney*, pp. 11–12.

17. Quoted in Benson, *Paul McCartney*, p. 16.

18. Beatles, *The Beatles Anthology*, p. 18.

19. Quoted in Ray Coleman, *McCartney: Yesterday . . . and Today*. Los Angeles: Dove Books, 1996, p. 28.

20. Quoted in Miles, *Paul McCartney*, p. 20.

21. Salewicz, *McCartney*, p. 4.

Chapter 2: All He Needed Was . . . Music

22. Beatles, *The Beatles Anthology*, p. 19.

23. Quoted in Benson, *Paul McCartney*, p. 26.

24. Coleman, *McCartney*, p. 31.

25. Quoted in Salewicz, *McCartney*, p. 34.

26. Quoted in Flippo, *Yesterday*, p. 20.

27. Quoted in Benson, *Paul McCartney*, p. 19.

28. Coleman, *McCartney*, p. 98.

29. Quoted in Miles, *Paul McCartney*, p. 40.

30. Quoted in Malcolm Doney, *Lennon and McCartney*. New York: Hippocrene Books, 1981, p. 7.

31. Quoted in Benson, *Paul McCartney*, p. 23.

32. Beatles, *The Beatles Anthology*, p. 12.

33. Quoted in Benson, *Paul McCartney*, p. 24.

34. Benson, *Paul McCartney*, p. 24.

Chapter 3: Paying His Dues

35. Flippo, *Yesterday*, pp. 39–40.

36. Quoted in Miles, *Paul McCartney*, p. 54.

37. Quoted in Miles, *Paul McCartney*, p. 58.

38. Quoted in Benson, *Paul McCartney*, p. 46.

39. Benson, *Paul McCartney*, p. 47.

40. Quoted in Miles, *Paul McCartney*, pp. 66–67.

41. Quoted in Benson, *Paul McCartney*, p. 56.

Chapter 4: Climbing the Ladder to Fame

42. Quoted in Doney, *Lennon and McCartney*, p. 23.

43. Quoted in Salewicz, *McCartney*, p. 105.

44. Flippo, *Yesterday*, p. 122.

45. Quoted in Flippo, *Yesterday*, p. 124.

46. Quoted in Miles, *Paul McCartney*, p. 81.

47. Quoted in Miles, *Paul McCartney*, p. 82.

48. Beatles, *The Beatles Anthology*, p. 96.

49. Beatles, *The Beatles Anthology*, p. 195.

50. Quoted in Miles, *Paul McCartney*, p. 37.

51. Quoted in Miles, *Paul McCartney*, p. 85.

52. Quoted in Ian MacDonald, *Revolution in the Head: The Beatles' Records and the Sixties*. New York: Henry Holt, 1994, p. 308.

53. Quoted in Benson, *Paul McCartney*, p. 78.

54. Beatles, *The Beatles Anthology*, p. 93.

55. Benson, *Paul McCartney*, p. 77.

56. Beatles, *The Beatles Anthology*, p. 356.

57. Quoted in Benson, *Paul McCartney*, p. 83.

58. Quoted in Miles, *Paul McCartney*, p. 103.

59. Beatles, *The Beatles Anthology*, p. 102.

60. Quoted in Geoffrey Giuliano, *Blackbird: The Life and Times of Paul McCartney*. New York: Dutton, 1991, p. 82.

61. MacDonald, *Revolution in the Head*, p. 316.

Chapter 5: Conquering the World with the Beatles

62. Quoted in Salewicz, *McCartney*, p. 160.

63. Quoted in Benson, *Paul McCartney*, p. 59.

64. Quoted in Ben Fong-Torres, "Yesterday, Today and Paul," *Rolling Stone*, June 17, 1976. www.rollingstone.com.

65. Beatles, *The Beatles Anthology*, p. 144.

66. Nicholas Schaffner, *The Beatles Forever*. Harrisburg, PA: Stackpole Books, 1977, p. 14.

67. Beatles, *The Beatles Anthology*, p. 109.

68. Quoted in John Blake, *All You Needed Was Love: The Beatles After the Beatles*. New York: Perigee Books, 1981, p. 162–163.

69. Quoted in Miles, *Paul McCartney*, p. 264.

70. Benson, *Paul McCartney*, p. 116.

71. Blake, *All You Needed Was Love*, p. 25.

72. Quoted in Benson, *Paul McCartney*, p. 135.

73. Quoted in Benson, *Paul McCartney*, p. 136.

74. Beatles, *The Beatles Anthology*, p. 220.

75. Beatles, *The Beatles Anthology*, p. 225.

76. Beatles, *The Beatles Anthology*, p. 226.

Chapter 6: Mantras, Money, Marriage, and McCartney's Mortality

77. Quoted in Miles, *Paul McCartney*, p. 303.

78. Benson, *Paul McCartney*, p. 143.

79. Beatles, *The Beatles Anthology*, p. 255.

80. Quoted in Benson, *Paul McCartney*, p. 161.

81. Beatles, *The Beatles Anthology*, p. 259.

82. Quoted in Miles, *Paul McCartney*, p. 400.

83. Quoted in Miles, *Paul McCartney*, p. 430.

84. Benson, *Paul McCartney*, p. 113.

85. Quoted in Benson, *Paul McCartney*, p. 196.

86. Quoted in Danny Fields, *Linda McCartney: A Portrait*. Los Angeles: Renaissance Books, 2000, p. 120.

87. Quoted in Miles, *Paul McCartney*, p. 517.

88. Flippo, *Yesterday*, p. 290.

89. Fields, *Linda McCartney*, p. 125.

90. Beatles, *The Beatles Anthology*, p. 340.

91. Fields, *Linda McCartney*, p. 105.

92. Quoted in Fields, *Linda McCartney*, p. 123.

93. Quoted in Benson, *Paul McCartney*, p. 213.

Chapter 7: One Door Closes, Another Opens

94. Quoted in Miles, *Paul McCartney*, p. 568.

95. Quoted in Benson, *Paul McCartney*, p. 217.

96. Quoted in Miles, *Paul McCartney*, p. 569.

97. Quoted in Ray Bonici, "Paul McCartney Wings It Alone," *Music Express*, April/May 1982. Reprinted (with a historical note by researcher

John Whelan), on the Ottawa Beatles Site, http://beatles.ncf.ca.

98. Fields, *Linda McCartney*, p. 144.

99. Quoted in Benson, *Paul McCartney*, p. 225.

100. Flippo, *Yesterday*, p. 320.

101. Quoted in Flippo, *Yesterday*, p. 320.

102. Quoted in Benson, *Paul McCartney*, p. 234.

103. Quoted in Fong-Torres, "Yesterday, Today and Paul."

104. Quoted in Fong-Torres, "Yesterday, Today and Paul."

105. Jeff Giles, "Lady McCartney: After an Astonishingly Loyal Twenty-Nine Years of Marriage, Paul Loses His Lovely Linda," *Newsweek*, May 4, 1998. www.newsweek.com.

106. Quoted in Miles, *Paul McCartney*, p. 525.

107. Giuliano, *Blackbird*, p. 312.

108. Quoted in Giuliano, *Blackbird*, p. 174.

109. Quoted in Fields, *Linda McCartney*, p. 182.

110. Quoted in Bonici, "Paul McCartney Wings It Alone."

111. Quoted in Jeff Giles, "The Music Man, the Family Man," *Newsweek*, October 23, 1995. www.newsweek.com.

Chapter 8: Spreading His Wings

112. Benson, *Paul McCartney*, p. 85.

113. Quoted in Steve Richards, "Beatles Fans Thought Him 'Cute'; He Saw Himself as Avant-Garde, Showing Lennon the Way. And Oasis, Who Adore Him? 'Really They Mean Nothing to Me,'" *New Statesman*, September 26, 1997. www.newstatesman.com.

114. McCartney, *Paintings*, p. 137.

115. Quoted in Paul McCartney, *Blackbird Singing: Poems and Lyrics, 1965–1999*. New York: W.W. Norton, 2001, p. 18.

116. McCartney, *Paintings*, p. 30.

117. McCartney, *Paintings*, p. 58.

118. Benson, *Paul McCartney*, p. 276.

119. Quoted in Salewicz, *McCartney*, p. 155.

120. Andrew Walker, "Sir Paul: Yesterday and Today," *BBC News*, December 20, 2002. www.bbc.co.uk.

121. Quoted in *BBC News*, "Sir Paul Made NYPD Detective," April 27, 2002. www.bbc.co.uk.

122. Quoted in Richards, "Beatles Fans Thought Him 'Cute.'"

For Further Reading

Books

Paul Dowswell, *Paul McCartney: An Unauthorized Biography.* Chicago: Heinemann Library, 2001. Intended for a middle school audience, this book provides a quick and clearly written overview of McCartney's life and work.

Bruce S. Glassman, *John Lennon and Paul McCartney: Their Magic and Their Music.* Woodbridge, CT: Blackbirch Press, 1995. The complex relationship of the world's most popular rock music composing team is explored in this excellent work.

Jorie B. Gracen, *Paul McCartney: I Saw Him Standing There.* New York: Billboard Books, 2000. Good information about McCartney's tours, essays by fans who have attended his concerts, and stunning images of McCartney are compiled by a photographer who covered his tours for many years.

R. Gary Patterson, *The Walrus Was Paul: The Great Beatle Death Clues.* New York: Simon and Schuster, 1998. Details of the "Paul is dead" incident are provided, along with descriptions of the death clues and in-depth cultural and literary analyses of the most bizarre event in Beatle history.

Adam Woog, *The Importance of the Beatles.* San Diego: Lucent Books, 1998. For young adult readers, this is the most comprehensive examination to date of the group that made Paul famous.

Periodical

Sue Arnold, "Roll Over, Beethoven," *Smithsonian,* January 1998.

Internet Sources

Jeff Giles, "The Music Man, the Family Man," *Newsweek,* October 23, 1995. www.newsweek.com

Paul Kennedy, "Tower's Heroes Reminded Me of Dad, Says Paul," *Liverpool Echo,* September 28, 2001. http://icliverpool.icnetwork.co.uk.

Video Recording

Paul McCartney, *Paul McCartney: In the World Tonight.* Los Angeles: Rhino Home Video, 1997.

Websites

MACCA Central (www.macca-central.com). This website, created by fans, includes information about Paul McCartney's tours, recordings, and other activities, along with extensive links to journals, magazines, and news services that carry current and archived articles about him.

MPL Communications, Inc. (www.mplcommunications.com). This official Paul McCartney website carries current press releases, information about tours and recordings, and a biography that is updated frequently.

Works Consulted

Books

Beatles, *The Beatles Anthology*. San Francisco: Chronicle Books, 2000. This massive collection of quotes and artwork by and about the Beatles is an invaluable source of primary information.

Ross Benson, *Paul McCartney: Behind the Myth*. London: Gollancz, 1992. This biography includes unflinching examinations of what, in the author's opinion, are flaws and contradictions in McCartney's character.

John Blake, *All You Needed Was Love: The Beatles After the Beatles*. New York: Perigee Books, 1981. During the decade after the Beatles broke up, each of the band members struggled to develop a new sense of identity, and this book describes their often painful efforts to be something besides former Beatles.

Ray Coleman, *McCartney: Yesterday . . . and Today*. Los Angeles: Dove Books, 1996. Many thoughtful insights about McCartney's songwriting are provided in this history and analysis of "Yesterday," his most famous song.

Malcolm Doney, *Lennon and McCartney*. New York: Hippocrene Books, 1981. Analyzing the relationship between Paul McCartney and John Lennon in the historical context of the 1960s and 1970s, the author strips away myths and presents a compelling story of two young men trying to maintain a friendship during exciting, but extremely stressful, times.

Danny Fields, *Linda McCartney: A Portrait*. Los Angeles: Renaissance Books, 2000. This biography by a rock music insider and longtime friend of Linda includes many valuable insights into Paul's life as a husband and father.

Chet Flippo, *Yesterday: The Unauthorized Biography of Paul McCartney*. New York: Doubleday, 1988. Although this biography seems harsh at times, the lively writing and colorful details make it accessible and engaging.

Geoffrey Giuliano, *Blackbird: The Life and Times of Paul McCartney*. New York: Dutton, 1991. The discography, event-by-event diary, and interviews at the end of this book are particularly engaging.

Mark Lewisohn, *The Beatles: Recording Sessions*. New York: Harmony Books, 1988. This is a complete account of what the Beatles did during each of their hundreds of recording sessions.

Ian MacDonald, *Revolution in the Head: The Beatles' Records and the Sixties*. New York: Henry Holt, 1994. This is the most thoughtful and in-depth analysis of the role of the Beatles' music in the profound cultural shift of the 1960s; the journal that juxtaposes Beatle history with scientific, literary, political, and musical history is outstanding.

Paul McCartney, *Blackbird Singing: Poems and Lyrics, 1965–1999.* New York: W.W. Norton, 2001. The introduction to this collection of McCartney's poetry and lyrics examines the importance of his writing.

————, *Paintings.* Boston: Little, Brown, 2000. Images of McCartney's most popular paintings are collected in this book, which also includes both an extensive interview with the author and excellent essays that examine his work in the context of contemporary art.

Barry Miles, *Paul McCartney: Many Years from Now.* New York: Henry Holt, 1997. Extensive quotes by McCartney gathered through many taped interviews and in-depth information based on the author's long friendship with him make this the most comprehensive current biography available.

Chris Salewicz, *McCartney: The Definitive Biography.* New York: St. Martin's, 1986. Although dated, this is an excellent source of information about McCartney's early years.

Nicholas Schaffner, *The Beatles Forever.* Harrisburg, PA: Stackpole Books, 1977. This collection of eyewitness accounts of performances by the Beatles, press reactions to the group, and Beatle memorabilia covers the period from 1964 to the breakup of the group.

Internet Sources

BBC News, "Sir Paul Made NYPD Detective," April 27, 2002. www.bbc.co.uk.

BBC News, "Sir Paul Unveils Heartfelt Painting," May 22, 2002. www.bbc.co.uk.

Ray Bonici, "Paul McCartney Wings It Alone," *Music Express*, April/May 1982. Reprinted (with a historical note by researcher John Whelan), on the Ottawa Beatles Site, http://beatles.ncf.ca.

Ben Fong-Torres, "Yesterday, Today and Paul," *Rolling Stone*, June 17, 1976. www.rollingstone.com.

Jeff Giles, "Lady McCartney: After an Astonishingly Loyal Twenty-Nine Years of Marriage, Paul Loses His Lovely Linda," *Newsweek*, May 4, 1998. www.newsweek.com.

Steve Richards, "Beatles Fans Thought Him 'Cute'; He Saw Himself as Avant-Garde, Showing Lennon the Way. And Oasis, Who Adore Him? 'Really They Mean Nothing to Me,'" *New Statesman*, September 26, 1997. www.newstatesman.com.

Timothy Tilghman, "Celebrating Freedom on a Global Scale: Paul McCartney Kicks Off Super Bowl XXXVI," *Rock on Tour*, February 2002. www.rockontour.net.

Laura Tuchman, Jan Herman, and Michael Ross (plus wire reports), "Star-Studded Show Staged as Tribute to Sept. 11 Heroes," *MSNBC. com*, October 21, 2001. www.msnbc.com.

Andrew Walker, "Sir Paul: Yesterday and Today," *BBC News*, December 20, 2002. www.bbc.co.uk.

Periodicals

Cathy Booth, "Paul at Fifty," *Time*, June 8, 1992.

Daily Mail, "But in New York Sir Paul Sings a Song of Freedom," October 20, 2001.

Becky Ebenkamp, "I Queried Paul," *Brandweek*, February 5, 2001.

Larry McShane, "Ono, McCartney Spar Again," *San Diego Union-Tribune*, December 20, 2002.

People Weekly, "Scoop," May 7, 2001.

Video Recording

The Beatles Anthology, 1996. Produced by Apple Corps. Turner Home Entertainment. Eight video cassettes.

Index

Picture Credits

Cover photo: © Hulton/Archive by Getty Images

© Bettman/CORBIS, 25

CBS/Landov, 61, 63

Bob Collier/Reuters/Landov, 13

© Hulton-Deutsch Collection/CORBIS, 49

© Hulton/Archive by Getty Images, 12, 15, 31, 35, 39, 45, 47, 64, 69, 73, 77, 85

Landov, 16

© Mitch McGeary, courtesy of Paul McCartney's Family Album (www.rarebeatles.com), 22, 74

Rafael Perez/Reuters/Landov, 51

Brad Rickerby/Reuters/Landov, 11

Darren Staples/Reuters/Landov, 88

Shannon Stapleton/Reuters/Landov, 93

Photofest, 21, 28, 42, 52, 55, 57, 60, 67, 71, 79, 80, 91, 92, 96

Steve Zmina, 18, 36, 83

About the Author

Kate Boyes is a migrant writer who roams the West in search of assignments. Her nature essays and poems appear in numerous journals and anthologies, and her travel writing is featured in Fodor's adventure guides about skiing, health resorts, Old West historic sites, and the Rocky Mountains. On her travels, she hikes, bikes, rafts white water, and gathers ideas for screenplays. When she is not on the road, she enjoys the peace and quiet of her off-the-grid cabin in Utah.